ACCOMPLISHING MORE WITH GOOGLE APPS

Pierre Khawand

Table of Contents

Introduction

Google Apps bring a whole new perspective for managing electronic communication and collaboration. It is a powerful environment that can help you revolutionize how you work. This book is intended to make your use of Google Apps highly effective and allow you to integrate the breakthrough Accomplishing More With Less Methodology, that has helped thousands of business professionals, into your daily work while leveraging the unique capabilities of Google Apps.

How to Get the Most Out Of This Book

If you are already comfortable with Google Apps, you can skip this introduction and proceed to chapter 1. If you are relatively new to Google Apps, and/or if would like to better understand the underlying concepts and their applications, then keep on reading. Overall, we recommend that you treat this book like a 'live' workshop and go through it at a pre-determined pace – such as one or two chapters per day or per week depending on your schedule, while doing the exercises along the way. We retain 10 to 20% of what we hear, 30% of what we see, and 70 to 90% of what we do. Doing is key.

If you cannot go through the exercises as described above, you can still get plenty of insights by simply reading the book or just referring to the topics that are of interest to you right now. Then you can visit other topics when they become more relevant and applicable to your needs. This "on an as-needed basis approach" is one of the concepts we promote in the Accomplishing More With Less Methodology. This approach can help us get started and reap immediate benefits instead of waiting for the right time to come and prolonging the current challenges and less-than-optimum conditions.

What will you be able to do as a result?

Here are some of the key benefits that our workshop participants report frequently:

- Better understand Google Apps features and benefits and become adept at leveraging them to increase your personal and group productivity.

- Better manage interruptions and stay focused on the task on hand until meaningful results are achieved while being responsive to the demands of your team and collaborate more effectively than ever before.

- Work more strategically instead of working harder, methodically manage competing priorities, and learn new and innovative tools that can help you better align your daily activities with your goals.

- Organize and manage your electronic and paper information easily and efficiently via a duplicate process that is practical and doable, instead of having your day "run over" by information and "low impact" activities.

- Manage stress like never before through purposeful action rather than passive reaction and turn stressful situations into opportunities.

- Understand the obstacles that are stopping you from reaching your desired accomplishments, and take the necessary actions that will lead to growth and transformation, and significantly increased fulfillment.

Google Apps in Action--Starting with Labels

Believe it or not, there are no folders[1]. Instead there are labels. You can create a set of labels and assign one or more labels to an e-mail message so you can more easily find the message later. Here is an example.

I receive this message from my colleague Daniella which relates to an important marketing initiative that we are collaborating on but the same message also includes some ideas relating to e-mail marketing technologies that can help us improve our future programs:

---

[1] Please note that Nested Labels that mimic folders are currently supported as discussed in chapter 8.

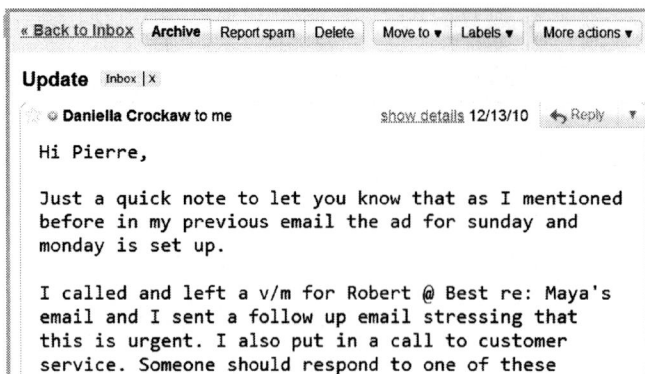

Figure 1: Sample e-mail message

After I reply to Daniella, I assign both the Marketing and Technology labels to the message and then archive it. This is easy to do using the Labels and Archive buttons shown above. In this case, these labels already exist because I created them previously in anticipation for their use:

Accounting
Administrative
Customers
Human Resources
Legal
Marketing
Marketing Online
Products
Prospects
Technology

Figure 2: Sample labels

If these labels didn't exist already, I can easily create them right when I need them by selecting the Create New menu option available from the Labels button. Labeling the message allows me to easily find it along with other similar messages. I click on the desired label in the Gmail screen and view all the related messages. For instance, I can easily see all the messages related to marketing by clicking on the Marketing label and all of the messages related to technology by clicking the Technology label. Incidentally, Daniella's message would appear in both of these views. You can see the advantage that labels have over traditional folders. With labels, we can easily assign more than one label to the same message and therefore easily find this message using any of the assigned labels.

What does Archive do anyway?

Clicking the Archive button removes the selected message from the inbox. The message is still available for viewing but not in the inbox. It is available in the All Mail label which is one of the standard labels in Gmail:

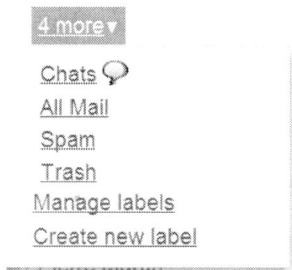

Figure 3: the All Mail label

The message is also available in any other label that you assigned to it. Most importantly it is available through the powerful search capability in Gmail.

Let us revisit the example above in which Daniella sent me an e-mail message to which I assigned both the Marketing and Technology labels and then archived it. I can find Daniella's message in any one of the following ways:

1. Clicking the All Mail label--typically you need to click the More label first (see below).
2. Clicking on one of the labels that I assigned to the message (in this case, Marketing, or Technology).
3. Searching for the message using words in the subject line, message content, or Daniella's name, among other things.

What does Move do?

Move is a shortcut for labeling and archiving. Let us say John sends me a message that is strictly about Technology. In this case, I would label it Technology and then archive it. Move will accomplish both of these steps at once. I click the

Move To button and select the Technology label from the popup list. As a result, the message is labeled Technology and archived at once.

Why use labels after all—knowing that I can easily search!

While search is very powerful and the ability to find messages when you need them is quite impressive in Gmail, labeling still has its benefits when it comes to the important messages. Later in the book, we will address this issues in more details (chapter 8), but for now let us take this example to illustrate the benefits of labeling.

Back to the message from John, let us say I didn't label this message and just archived it hoping that I can rely on search to find it if/when I need it. A few months go by and the need to search for this message comes up. For search to provide me with the desired result quickly and easily, ***I need to remember enough about the message*** to be able to search for it, such as the sender, the timeframe, and/or specific keywords relating to the subject line or the content.

If I happen to remember that John was the sender and the approximate time frame or more specifically what was mentioned in the message, then search will do the job! However, if many people sent me messages about this same topic and if these conversations took place over a long period of time and included a large volume of messages, the result set from the search may be too large and finding John's message may take a long time and sometimes not conclude successfully. In this case, if I had labeled John's message, the label would have located the message more easily assuming I only label important and relevant messages. Later in the book we discuss the 80/20 rule and recommend labeling only the top 20% of messages—those that are critical to the results that we are trying to accomplish.

Conversations in Action

Gmail by default groups all the messages within the same e-mail conversation (i.e. related to the same topic) together so that the whole conversation appears as one item in the inbox. For instance here are e-mail conversations containing 5, 4, and 5 messages respectively:

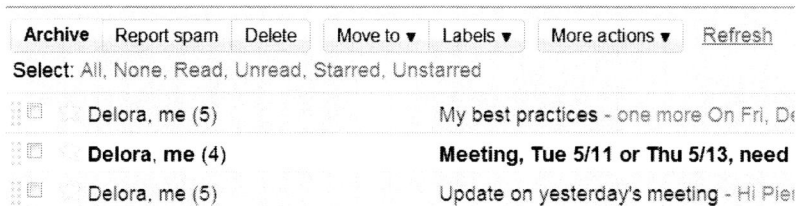

Figure 9: Conversations in Gmail

When you click on a conversation, it expands and displays the details of the underlying messages such as:

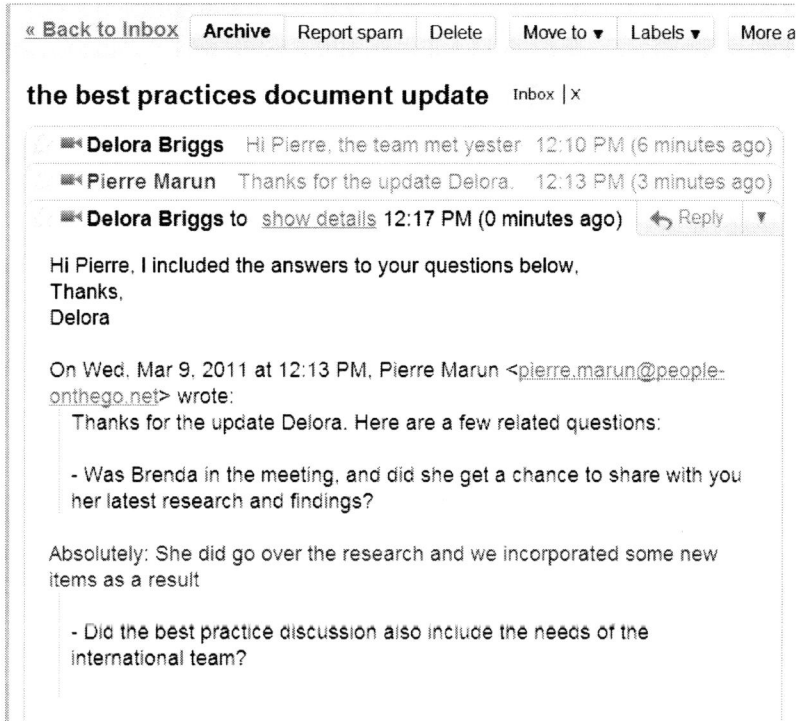

Figure 10: Expanded conversation in Gmail

"Smart" Conversations

Gmail conversations are what I call "smart" conversations because they have some built-in intelligence and are designed to help us more easily manage the conversations. If you wondered for instance when you looked at the conversation above (Figure 10) why the third message was expanded and the first two messages were collapsed, that was for a good reason. That was because I have already read the first two messages. Gmail expands the message that is still unread which is the third message in this case. Therefore, when these conversations grow and accumulate new messages, fear not! When you click on the conversation, it will automatically expand and show you the most logical message--the first unread message.

Another helpful aspect of conversations relates to the order in which they are displayed in Gmail. Not only are they displayed in reserve chronological order with the most recent on top, but also when a new message arrives which relates to an older conversation, the whole conversation is brought back to the top showing the newly received message in bold. Clicking on the conversation will immediately display the first unread message in the conversation. In a world that is characterized by e-mail overload, conversations help keep relevant information together and well under control, instead of adding more items to our already overloaded inboxes.

Search is just as intelligent! When searching within conversations, only the messages that contain the search keywords are expanded with the occurrences of the search keywords highlighted.

Collapsing, expanding, printing, and forwarding

To help you easily manage conversations, Gmail offers several useful functions including the following:

New window

Print all

Expand all

Forward all

Figure 11: Managing conversations

"Expand all" expands all the messages in the current conversation so you can easily scroll down and see the content of each message. When you expand all messages, this command turns into "Collapse all" and allows you to quickly collapse the conversation so you can only see the headers and locate a specific message and click on it to expand it.

Print all and forward all can be very helpful when reviewing conversations or wanting to communicate conversations or selected excerpts from the conversation to others, or copy and paste these excerpts into other documents.

Still not convinced about conversations? You can turn them off!

Occasionally we encounter users who are not initially fond of conversations and want to have their e-mail messages displayed separately similar to what they are used to in other e-mail applications. Typically I ask them a simple question that goes a long way in convincing them otherwise: "Do you really want to have the 10 or 20 or more e-mail messages that went back and forth about the same topic clutter your inbox by showing up as 10 or 20 or more separate line items scattered throughout your inbox?" In other words, "Wouldn't it be easier if your 100 or 200 e-mail messages that you get every day show up as 30 to 50 conversations that are easier to wrap your arms around and manage?"

I also use the analogy of taking a book, separating the book chapters, and mixing them with unrelated chapters from other unrelated books. Would you ever do such a thing? Of course not! So why would you want to separate your e-mail conversations, which are in essence "micro" books, and have their chapters (the individual e-mail messages) mixed with other unrelated chapters (other e-mail messages)? Wouldn't that be adding more chaos to an already busy and hectic inbox?

Most users are convinced of the benefits of conversations right away or get used to them and start to appreciate the advantages they bring soon after they start to use Gmail. However if you happen to still prefer to have your individual e-mail messages show up separately instead of being grouped together in conversations, you can disable this feature by going to the E-Mail Settings, then in the General tab, and set the conversation view to off:

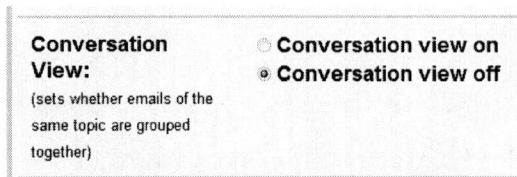

Conversation View:
(sets whether emails of the same topic are grouped together)

○ **Conversation view on**
◉ **Conversation view off**

Figure 12: Turning conversation view off

E-mail Tasks in Action

In today's information overload, managing e-mail is a significant and multi-faceted challenge, which we will be addressing one facet at a time throughout the book. For now let us focus on the unique challenge of managing tasks that come to us through e-mail, which I call "e-mail tasks." These e-mails include information about tasks that will take time to perform. These are different from the regular e-mails which we simply reply to, answer questions, express opinions, communicate decisions, and provide information that is readily available.

Using email alone to track e-mail tasks and manage them is not likely to serve us well because:

a) The e-mail inbox does not show us *how much time* it would take to do these tasks, and therefore we have no idea on how busy or committed we are.

b) The e-mail inbox does not tell us *when* to do these tasks and therefore does not help us with our task planning.

c) The e-mail inbox does not remind us about upcoming tasks and therefore we need to review these e-mails frequently to make sure we are not missing important deadlines.

Rather than using the e-mail inbox to track and manage these tasks, it would be more effective to schedule them on our calendar or add them to our to-do lists. Google Apps easily allow us to turn such e-mails into Calendar events or tasks and therefore have them clearly identified, better accounted for (and visually accounted for in the case of the Calendar), and better monitored with the necessary reminders and notifications.

Turning an e-mail into a Calendar Event

When you receive an e-mail about an important task, and you decide to add this task to your calendar so you can reserve time for it, click on the More Actions button in the Gmail screen:

Figure 4: the More Actions button

Select the "Create event" option and the following screen opens and allows you to enter the details of the task, including allocating the appropriate time, and setting the appropriate reminders:

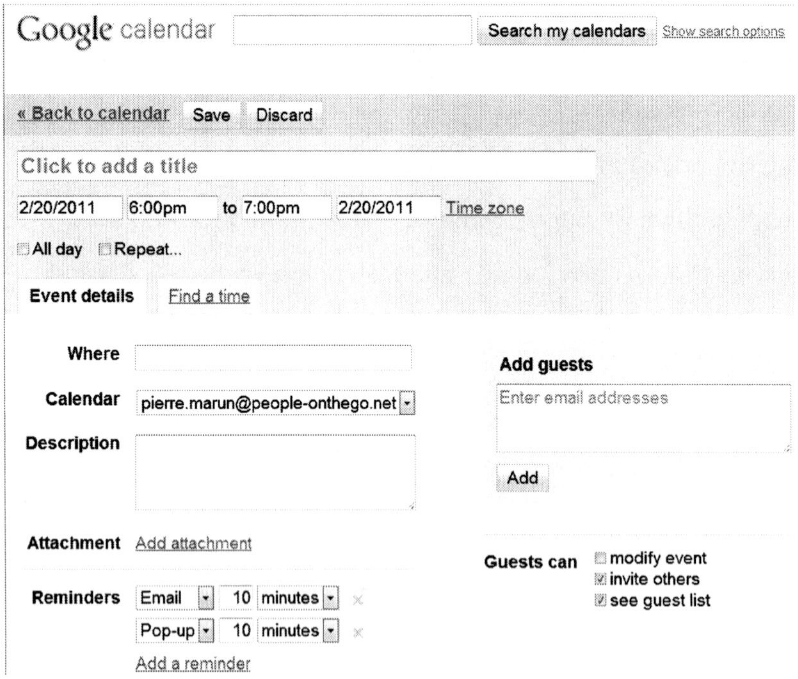

Figure 5: Sample Calendar event screen

Turning an e-mail into a task

When you receive an e-mail about an important task, and you decide to add this task to your task list so that it is easier to track and manage with other tasks, click on the More Actions button in the Gmail screen (see figure 4 above) and select the "Add to Tasks" option. The following screen opens and allows you to see the newly created task in the task list.

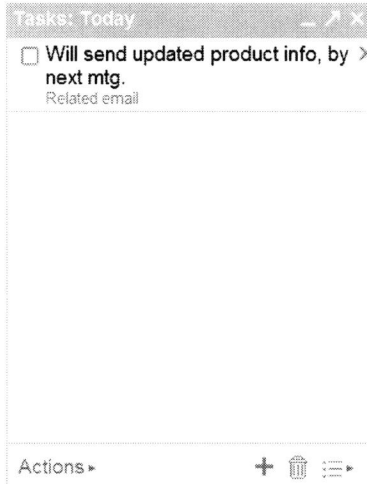

Figure 6: Task list

Clicking on the arrow to the right of the task will display the details of the task and allows you to set a due date, add notes, and also assign the task to a specific task list if you have multiple lists, among other things.

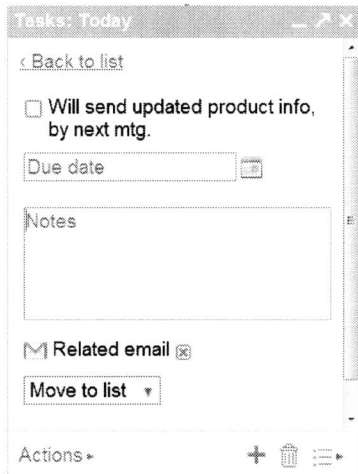

Figure 7: Task details

Time sensitive e-mail tasks

One of the advantages that the Calendar events offer is the ability to setup a variety of notifications to remind you of the events. When you create a Calendar event to track and manage an e-mail task or any e-mail as a matter of fact, you can take advantage of these reminders and not miss time sensitive items. Here is an example of the variety of reminders that you can set. In this case I have multiple reminders that include a text message to a mobile device in case I happen to be away from e-mail:

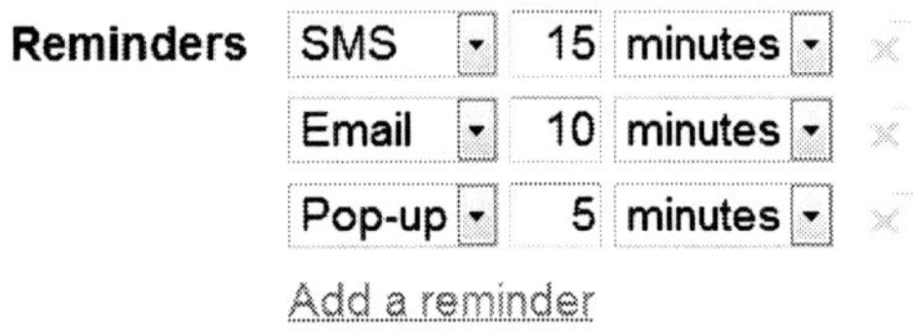

Figure 8: Calendar event reminders

To use text messaging, you need to complete the Mobile Setup which is part of the Calendar Settings:

Figure 8: Mobile Setup in the Calendar Settings

Chat in Action

Chat allows you to easily communicate in real time with other users[2]. This can be either someone on the same Google Apps installation, but not necessarily. You can allow the contacts that you communicate with often to chat with you without having to get your prior approval or you can require approval. Chat is located on the left side of the Gmail screen and can be expanded to show you the list of users you are connected with and their status:

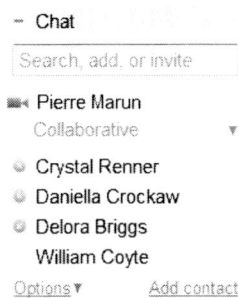

Figure 13: Chat list

The green color next to Delora's name (not visible though in the black and white picture) indicates that she is online and available to chat. When you move the mouse over her name in the chat list shown above, you get a popup window indicating her status and allowing you to e-mail her, chat with her, or video chat with her. Clicking on the Chat button opens the Chat window and allows us to type our message and send it:

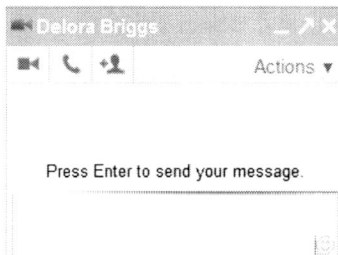

Figure 14: Chat window

---

[2] If the user you want to chat with is not online, you can still send your message and it will be delivered to them the next time they are online.

Delora will see our message popup on her screen and can then engage in the chat conversation by responding to our message with a chat message. Delora can alternatively respond to the chat message via e-mail, voice, or video, as illustrated in Figure 15 above. The chat window allows her to do more than just text chat. It allows her to switch to voice chat, video chat, and add additional people to our chat session

A few more chat capabilities that are worth mentioning include a) the chat history, when enabled, allows us to view and search previous chat messages and b) the ability to chat off record so that a particular chat conversation is not saved. Enabling and disabling the chat history is done from the Chat tab in the E-mail Settings:

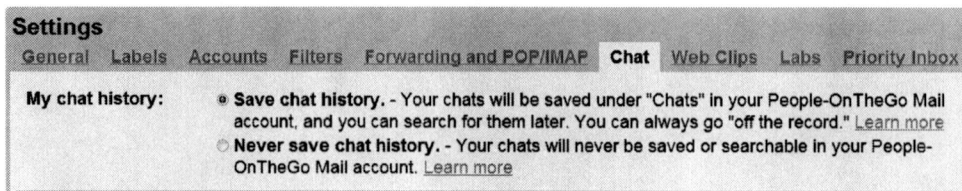

Settings

General Labels Accounts Filters Forwarding and POP/IMAP **Chat** Web Clips Labs Priority Inbox

My chat history: ● **Save chat history.** - Your chats will be saved under "Chats" in your People-OnTheGo Mail account, and you can search for them later. You can always go "off the record." Learn more
○ **Never save chat history.** - Your chats will never be saved or searchable in your People-OnTheGo Mail account. Learn more

Figure 15: Chat history settings

Using Chat to have real time conversations can largely increase individual and group productivity and save everyone involved many back and forth e-mail messages. Chat is also used to check-in with others about their availability and potentially switching to voice or video to conduct a more elaborate real time conversation.

Using chat excessively however can be interruptive. Chat is also not ideal for long and complex discussions. Therefore it is recommended to use chat selectively depending on the situation at hand.

Integrated E-mail, Chat, Voice, and Video for streamlining communication

The integrated chat, voice, and video allow us to streamline communication and make collaboration easy and efficient instead of relying primarily on e-mail. Having worked with thousands of business professionals from a variety of companies ranging from startups to global companies, what I see in the workplace more often than not is that e-mail is overused and abused, and consequently, it results in great inefficiencies that lead to substantial opportunity cost. It is said that when you have a hammer everything looks like a nail. We have the hammer, and in this case it is called "e-mail" and every communication looks like an e-mail message. E-mail is easy. It is quick. It has no hard costs associated with it (only inefficiencies and opportunity cost which tend to go unnoticed). In addition, we allow ourselves to say whatever we want in an e-mail message and not get interrupted by someone else's point of view (which can be rewarding but dangerous). It is no wonder we are so quick to use e-mail in almost any situation.

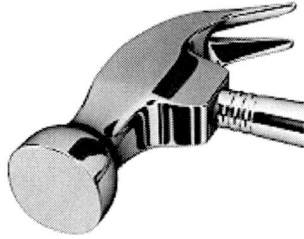

Blinded by the ease and speed of e-mail, among other factors, we tend to forget that e-mail is only one of many tools for communicating. Below is a list of some of the tools that can largely benefit us when used appropriately in conjunction with e-mail.

Use this opportunity to reflect on what each tool is ideal for and not so ideal for, and jot down your answers in the table below before comparing them to the suggested answers:

	Ideal for	Not so ideal for
E-mail		
Chat		
Voice Calls		
Web Conferencing		
Video Calls		
In-Person		

Here are some suggested answers for you to consider:

	Ideal for	Not so ideal for
E-mail	Factual/Asynchronous	Emotional issues
Chat	Quick exchanges	Long/complex issues
Voice Calls	Discussions	Visuals
Web Conferencing	Screen sharing	Interacting/seeing people
Video Calls	Seeing people	Data/Factual/Quick
In-Person	Complex/Emotional	Remote people

The integrated e-mail, chat, voice, and video in Google Apps can help us switch between these modes of communication seamlessly and on demand based on the needs of the situation at hand. This makes communication a dynamic process and puts us in control instead of being at the mercy of the technology. In addition, and as we will explore later in this chapter and further in the book, Google Docs allow us to share documents in real time, therefore mimicking screen sharing and enabling us to collaborate like never before!

Calendar in Action

Calendaring is made easy in Google Apps. In addition to the easy user interface and typical features you would expect such as adding calendar events, inviting others, adding notes and attachments, setting recurring events, and setting reminders, you can enable the Mobile Setup in the Calendar Settings as mentioned above and therefore send your important reminders as text messages to your mobile phone. This is very handy for people who find themselves often on the go and yet needing to stay alert and not miss a beat.

You can also create multiple calendars and assign different names and colors to these calendars. For instance, if you happen to manage the marketing events for your team or company, create a separate calendar for these events and assign it a color that is different from your primary calendar so you can easily see these events without having them clutter your own calendar and also make it difficult for people to find available time on your calendar.

Another application for multiple calendars might be to have your main calendar dedicated to meetings that you have with others, and yet another calendar dedicated for blocking times for important tasks that you want to accomplish, and yet another for important follow-ups that you want to handle at certain times. Although this is not how we traditionally use the calendar, as we will explore further in chapter 6, this can be one of the powerful techniques for managing important tasks and follow-ups and bringing them to the forefront instead of having them buried in e-mail messages and task lists.

The calendars you create appear in the calendar section on the left as shown below:

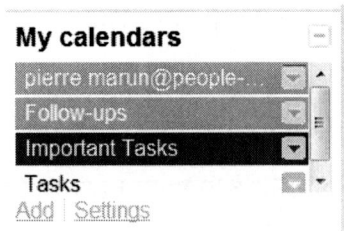

My calendars

pierre.marun@people-...

Follow-ups

Important Tasks

Tasks

Add | Settings

Figure 16: Calendar list

Clicking on the arrow next to a calendar allows you to hide or display the calendar, change its setting, as well as share it with others as described below:

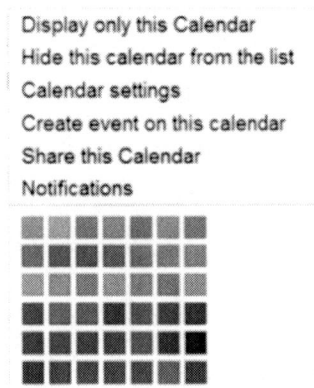

Display only this Calendar

Hide this calendar from the list

Calendar settings

Create event on this calendar

Share this Calendar

Notifications

Figure 17: Calendar list

Calendar Sharing

Calendar sharing allows you to share your calendar with other users. You can make your calendar public, or share your calendar with users in your organization, or even limit the sharing to users that you specify. You can also share the details or just show only the free/busy times without sharing the details:

Figure 18: Calendar sharing

Google Docs in Action

Google Docs allow you to create and manage a variety of documents including presentations, spreadsheets, forms, and more!

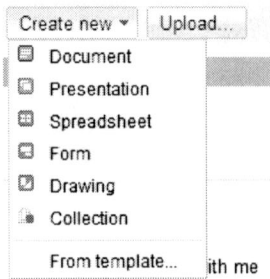

Figure 19: Types of documents in Google Docs

If you already have documents that were created with other applications such as Microsoft Office, you can import your existing documents into Google Docs. You can also export Google Docs documents in a variety of formats.

Google Docs allow you to easily share documents with others and co-create content in real time. We will be discussing Google Docs later in the book in addition to providing practical examples throughout the book on how to leverage their capabilities. For now, here is an example of how my colleague Jenny Blake and I used Google Docs to plan and manage a webinar series that we conducted.

Using Google Docs to collaborate and co-create

Jenny Blake, author of *Life After College*[3], has been a guest speaker at several of my company's Lunch and Learn Webinars covering a variety of workplace issues relating to Gen Y, Social Media, the e-mail overload, career management, and the release of her book, among others. Planning and coordinating these webinars involved sharing information, discussing options, creating content, exchanging lots of ideas and making numerous decisions along the way. This process would typically involve dozens if not hundreds of e-mail conversations and an equally large number of attachments, and not to mention the inefficiency and confusion relating to managing these attachments via e-mail. But not in our case!

---

[3] Life After College —The Complete Guide to Getting What You Want (www.lacbook.com)

Our effort involved very few e-mails and was mostly managed through Google Docs. The process would start with a live discussion of the goal and strategy of the webinar at hand while we simultaneously document our discussion in a Google Docs document in real time. The rest is history!

We continue to expand on these initial discussions individually and detail the content and logistics as we each come up with new ideas and new content. Every time I visit the document, I see the latest additions from Jenny, and vice versa. We effortlessly leverage each other's work and build on each other's ideas. There was never confusion about which version is the latest or who changed what! Occasionally, when we have a live discussion (mostly by phone), we would be working off of the same document and editing it simultaneously in real time. No need for an e-mail to summarize the notes from our live session or to send the latest version of the document. These were practices from the past and now with Google Docs we can move into a whole new era of collaboration and co-creation!

Labs, Gadgets, Priority Inbox and more!

There is much more to Gmail and Google Apps which we will be addressing later in the book. Labs, Gadgets, and Priority Inbox are examples of additional capabilities that can be enabled to help you expand your use of Gmail and Google Apps in a variety of ways. Here is the Labs tab is the Mail Settings for instance:

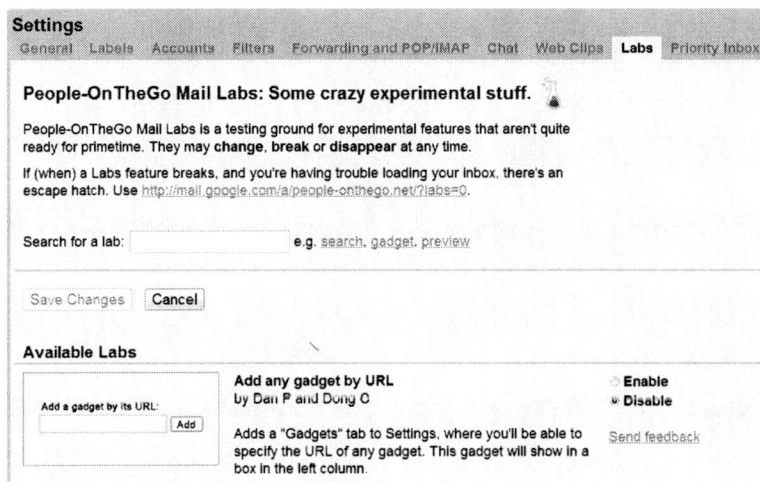

Figure 20: The Labs in Mail Settings

It is about time!

Now that you have seen some of the key concepts in Google Apps, and know there is more to come, we are ready to dive into some of the key productivity concepts in the Accomplishing More With Less Methodology and show you more specifically how Google Apps can help you master these breakthrough practices and revolutionize how you manage your time, your e-mail, your information, your priorities, and accomplish much more in a lot less time, less effort, and less stress. And for those who are interested in helping others accomplish more with less, or in other productivity topics, below is some additional information.

Becoming Certified

If you happen to be part of the training and development group at your organization and would like to help your users take their productivity to the next level, you can join our certification program. For more information on how to get certified, training@people-onthego.com

Gift Certificate for an Online Live Workshop

When you purchase this book, you are entitled to a gift certificate that enables you to attend one of our 90-minute or 2-hour online live workshops for a nominal registration fee of $10 (the regular fees for these workshops either $69 or $99). These workshops cover a variety of productivity topics and workplace issues. You can review the schedule at www.people-onthego.com/webinars

To claim your gift certificate, please e-mail the proof of purchase of your book (the online receipt) to training@people-onthego.com and include "Book gift certificate" in the subject line.

Staying in touch

We invite you to join us and become part of the Accomplishing More With Less community, which includes thousands of professionals who want to be more effective and more fulfilled at work and beyond, as well as contribute more fully to their organizations and to their communities. Here are ways in which you can become part of this community:

- Join the "Accomplishing more with less group" on Facebook
- Join the "Accomplishing more with less group" on LinkedIn
- Join our complimentary lunch & learn webinars every Thursday at noon Pacific Time. See the full program and registration information at: www.people-onthego.com/free-webinars
- Connect with me on Twitter (@pierrekhawand)

Congratulations

Congratulations for choosing to be part of the Accomplishing More With Less movement and Google Apps. Your exciting and fulfilling journey has just begun!

Chapter 1: The Myth of Multitasking—focus to get results

The digital revolution should make us all incredibly efficient and productive. The tools at our fingertips — easy multimedia production software, instant and free communication around the globe, massive research power without needing to get up out of our chair — should allow us to complete tasks in hours instead of days and leave us more leisure time than we could ever have imagined. And yet this promise of efficiency seems to be just a little beyond where we are right now, somehow always eluding our grip. We can't seem to get there.

Our work environment is one of great onslaught. We struggle to get done on Friday what we had hoped to achieve the previous Monday. Why is it so difficult to do the things we really want to do? Keep on reading!

The Results Curve™

Let us start by examining how our results change with time when we are working on a task. In an ideal world, when we start to work on a task, we start to produce results, and then as we continue to work on that task, we produce more results. This continues until eventually the flow of results begins to level off and start to diminish. Results diminish because we get tired or saturated, or because we have done what we could and now need to wait for someone else to do their part, or because we have completed the task. The graph below (the Results Curve™) illustrates this progression:

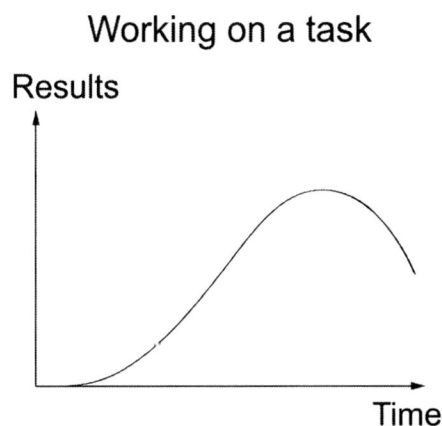

Working on a task

Now let's get back to *real* life. What happens in the real world after we spend a few minutes on a task?

We get interrupted!

E-mail arrives in our inbox and we feel this irresistible urge to check it out, or a chat message pops up with a compelling proposition. Then there's the phone ringing or a chatty colleague or eager boss stopping by. When an interruption takes place, it prematurely ends the progress on the task at hand as shown in the graph below:

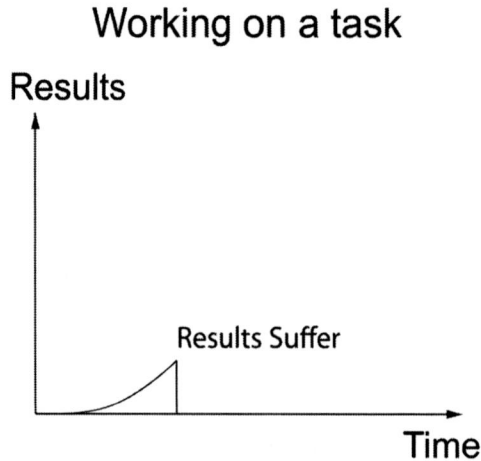

Working on a task

Results

Results Suffer

Time

Post-interruption, when we resume our work on this task, are we going to start at the same level where we left off? Unfortunately not! Our mind needs to re-retrieve the relevant pieces of information that were let go of during the interruption and reconstruct the logic and relationships that were previously established. This means we will suffer a setback at the restarting point as shown below.

Working on a task

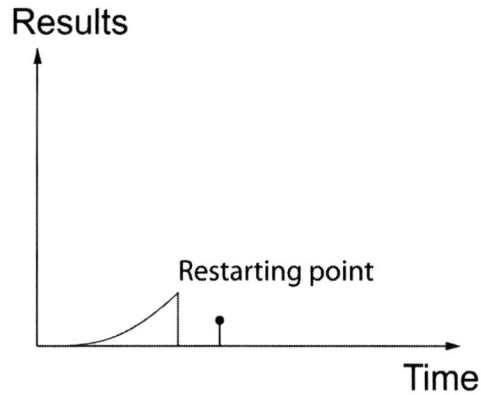

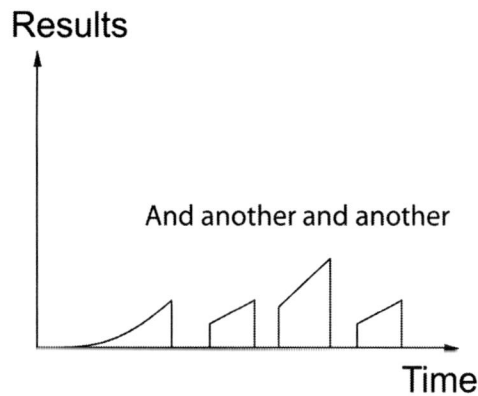

Results

Restarting point

Time

We start making progress again, but a few minutes later, another interruption pulls us off task, and our results suffer again. This pattern repeats itself time after time as the calls, emails, and chat messages continue. Interruptions are no longer the exceptions in the digital age – they are the norm. The graph below illustrates this phenomenon. This is our life: a life of interruptions.

Working on a task

Results

And another and another

Time

A Life of Interruptions

If we compare the actual results that we are getting, represented by the shaded areas in the graph below, to the potential results that we could realize if we could manage to focus on one task, represented by that beautiful uninterrupted Results Curve™, the outcome is nothing less than shocking:

Working on a task

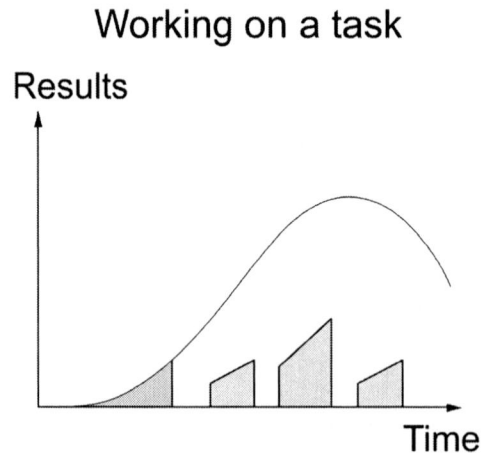

Our life has become a series of frequent interruptions intermingled with small bursts of work in which our ability to achieve anything of quality has been highly diluted. We are preventing ourselves from reaching the potential results area in the graph by letting interruptions take us off track and deprive us from using our gifts.

The Myth of Multi-Tasking

While some of us take pride in our ability to handle multiple tasks at the same time, and even believe that we are actually accomplishing more as we multitask, in reality there is no such a thing as true multi-tasking when it comes to the human mind. What we are really doing is task switching. Yes, some of us who are highly gifted can walk and chew gum at the same time. But those are autonomous functions — something that goes on in the autonomous part of our nervous system. It's our brain's ability to digest our food without asking us to think about it, or the part that keeps us breathing even though we're fast asleep. But when it comes to the limitations of our conscious brain, we cannot do two demanding things at once. Sorry, but there it is.

The cost of task switching is immense. In addition to the tangible cost of time, and the less tangible but significant opportunity cost, we also suffer individually and collectively from increased stress and less than satisfying work conditions as we race from one thing to another all day long and generally feel at the end of the day that we haven't actually accomplished much at all.

The Accomplishment Zone™

Accomplishments don't come from working a few minutes here and there. Accomplishments come from those periods in which we have the opportunity to engage in focused and purposeful work. In order to accomplish meaningful results, we must stay focused long enough to reach the area of greater results in the Results Curve™ before we switch to another task or allow ourselves to be interrupted. This is the Accomplishment Zone™.

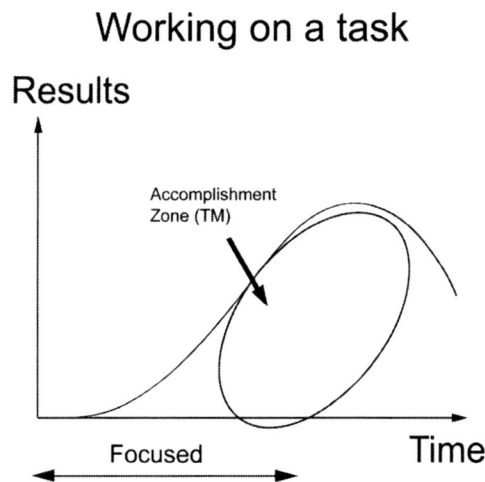

Working on a task

In the Accomplishment Zone™ we allow ourselves to experience deep thinking and creative problem solving. Here is where our brains can use their awesome power to discover hidden relationships between the parts as well as new and creative insights about the whole. This is where we can solve tough problems. This is where breakthroughs lie!

How Much Uninterrupted Time is Enough?

For most of our challenging work, it will be valuable for us to choose a consistent target time period that will get us into the Accomplishment Zone™ on a regular basis. In our workshops we've had participants indicate a preference for a 30 minute work period, while others want an entire hour. My suggestion is that we aim for an uninterrupted 40 minute period. My belief after working with thousands of people on productivity issues and challenges is that while 30 minutes is reasonable and achievable, after 30 minutes of focused work, the "engine" is now fully warmed up and functioning optimally, so those extra 10 minutes are "pure" performance. Those 10 minutes are all in the high-potential area. We must grab them while we can.

Working on a task

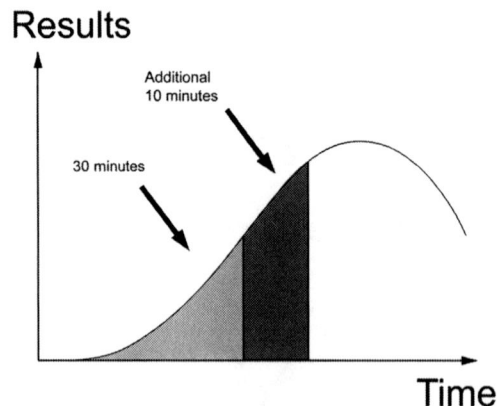

The Collaboration Zone™

When we create our Accomplishment Zone™, we block out interruptions great and small, including those that come from others in our work group. How do we make sure though that our own high performance time doesn't come at the expense of others?

After our highly focused session, in which we've "turned the world off" and focused on one important task, it will be time to switch gears and "turn the world on" again and engage into our collaborative activities. This is the Collaboration Zone™.

In the Collaboration Zone™, we handle e-mail messages, check voice messages, answer chat messages, and make ourselves available for virtual and in-person interactions. The Collaboration Zone™ can even include a social or private break. The collaborative session can be 10, 15, 30 minutes, or even longer, depending on how much collaborative work is necessary.

Working on a task

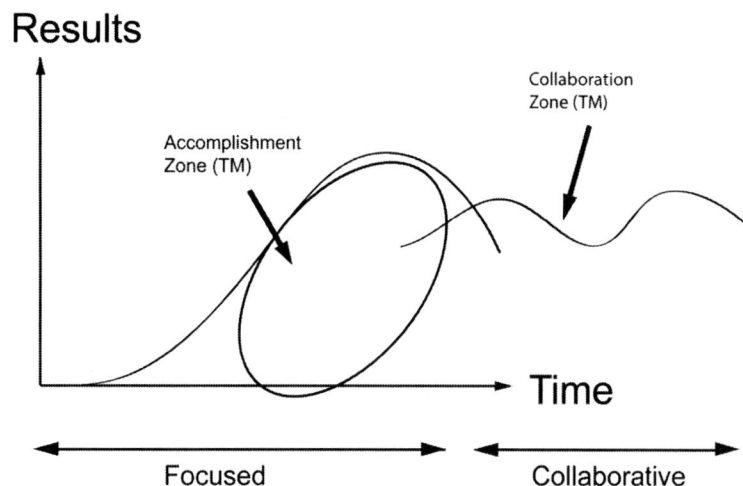

Results

Accomplishment Zone (TM)

Collaboration Zone (TM)

Time

Focused   Collaborative

The Collaboration Zone™, shown in the graph above, is just as important as the Accomplishment Zone™. Together they satisfy the need to accomplish individual tasks and the need to connect and collaborate with the rest of the world. They help us resolve this ongoing conflict between focus and connectivity.

The collaborative session can also be energizing and enriching as we find out what went on out there while we were focusing on an individual task. It also brings a healthy dose of realism as we observe and collect data from an ever-changing environment. It helps us get back to our next focused session with a higher level of enthusiasm and better perspective. The collaborative session, together with the focused session, are the yin and yang of success in today's workplace.

The Killer Bs

What are the interruptions that keep us out of the Accomplishment Zone™? Our workshop participants are quick to point out e-mail, IM, phone calls, people dropping by, and our need or desire to take all sorts of breaks. But let's assume that we have all of these under control (which we will address soon and throughout this book). Let's say we've got a system for our e-mail and other digital interrupters. We've got a sign up so no one drops in on us. The phone is taking messages. So we're safe as far as these potential interruptions are concerned. Now are we going to be in the Accomplishment Zone™ without interruption for 40 minutes?

Well, not exactly. That is because none of the above mentioned interruptions capture the single and most noteworthy enemy of us successfully controlling our precious 40 minutes. There's one interrupter left, and it doesn't come from the outside. This interruption is our own wandering thoughts. The #1 killer of the Accomplishment Zone™ is us! Our own wandering thoughts are by far the primary cause for interrupting our current task and derailing us into new and often unrelated territories.

Thoughts are powerful. Thoughts can be valuable and relevant to the task at hand. We need those thoughts to do our work – to imagine, to evaluate, to think and create. But the way our minds naturally work means that our thoughts aren't always directed to the task at hand. When our thoughts help our work, we are controlling them. When our thoughts take us away from our work, they are controlling us.

Imagine me working on budget projections for the quarter. As I try to think about how much I should allow for online advertisement, my gaze drifts up as I contemplate what the right number might be. My gaze settles on the photo on my desk. Me in Paris. What a lovely trip that was last year. Except for the price of gas. I can remember that gas station where I stopped to fill up. I can see the numbers flashing past 90 euros. No question Hertz should be renting hybrids or electrics. I then start browsing the internet to see if anyone is renting hybrids in Europe.

I've gone from the photo lying on my desk, to browsing the Internet for the next 10 to 20 minutes. It is not inconceivable that while browsing the Internet, I notice that a new e-mail has arrived in my inbox. I hear the beep and take a look at the new e-mail message and start to reply to it. Meanwhile, I glance at the spam filter folder, and notice that there are number of new messages there. I abandon the e-mail message and start going through my spam filter. Another 10 or 20 minutes go by. Suddenly I realize that I am way off track, and ask myself the question "What the heck was I working on?"

Focusing on Task A

I call the work we are trying to accomplish Task A. Task A represents the work that is our most important work. It's what we want to do. It's what our team wants us to do, too. If we do all our Task As, we accomplish all of our life's desire. Accomplishment lies in racking up those Task As. Ideally, in the Accomplishment Zone™, we would focus on Task A and perform activities related to Task A until Task A is finished or until we've at least made significant progress on it.

In essence, our well-behaved mind would have thoughts related to Task A which are shown in the diagram below as Thoughts A1, A2, and A3.

Our mind working on a task (Task A)

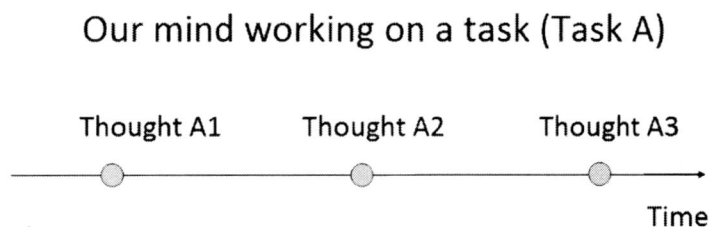

Thought A1   Thought A2   Thought A3

Time

Promoting Killer B

Unfortunately, reality tends to be a little different from this ideal. Typically, soon after we start working on Task A, Thought B comes along. What in the world is Thought B doing here? Who knows, but it's here. What do we do when thought B comes along?

As shown below, more often than not, when Thought B comes along, we are likely to get kidnapped by it. We shift our line of thinking to Thought B while abandoning Task A. Thought B is a threat to continuing to work on our goal which is Task A. Thought B is dangerous. Thought B is in fact, a Killer B. Seriously — a kind of thought so bad we call it a "killer?" Yes. It's that bad.

Thought B pops up in our mind

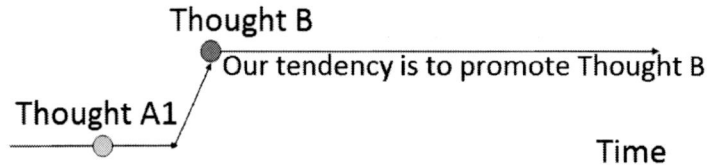

Thought B

Our tendency is to promote Thought B

Thought A1

Time

When we give our attention to Thought B and begin to think about what it means, and begin to make associations for it, and begin to play with it, we let Thought B take over our consciousness. Until we can regain control of our senses, we have abandoned work on Thought A and Task A.

Capturing Killer B

What options do we have other than promoting Killer B? What would be a more constructive option? We could "capture" Killer B, so we can free our mind from it and return to it later if necessary.

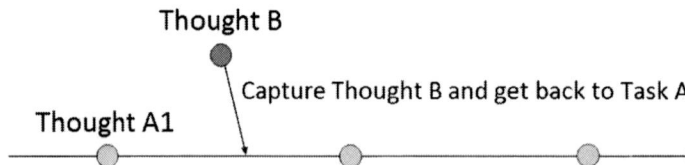

Thought B

Capture Thought B and get back to Task A

Thought A1

Where do we capture Killer B? On the "Capture" page in a valuable tool I will introduce shortly: a paper journal. The primary purpose of the "Capture" page is to capture Killer Bs as quickly as possible and return to the task at hand.

Paper. How analog. Why not capture Killer B in electronic format? Why not file it where it belongs right away? Isn't this what the "touch once" theory has been promoting in the workplace for years?

The problem with capturing the errant thought in an electronic format is that it takes too much time. It pulls us away from Task A long enough to truly derail us. This would be the equivalent of reinforcing Killer B. If we truly believe that Task A is important, and we are serious about getting into the Accomplishment Zone™, we want to spend the least amount of time on getting Killer B out of the way. We live in a different time environment that requires different measures. We are no longer talking in terms of minutes but of seconds.

This means there is no time for opening or activating a desktop application, accessing the Web, using a stylus or touch screen, organizing, prioritizing, or philosophizing. There is only time to capture 3 to 5 key words, in 3 to 5 seconds, on the one and only Capture page, in the one and only paper journal, by the one and only *me*, in my own handwriting that no one else needs to understand. The Capture page in the paper journal is the path to the Accomplishment Zone™.

Ignoring Killer B

Are all thoughts worth capturing? Thankfully not. Otherwise, some of us would spend most of our time capturing the multitude of thoughts that keep popping up into our busy and creative minds.

If we determine that Killer B is just a random thought and is not worth capturing because its future value is insignificant, it makes more sense to ignore it and get back to task A as soon as possible, as illustrated below:

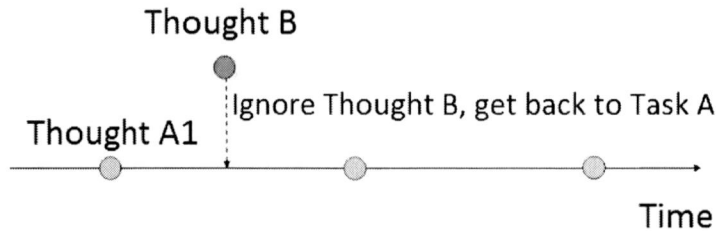

Thought B

Ignore Thought B, get back to Task A

Thought A1

Time

Turning Killer B into Useful B

It is possible that Killer B proves not to be a "killer" after all. It may be that Killer B has some value to add to Task A. This is actually the way our mind works sometimes. It unexpectedly brings an interesting thought that may not be directly related to Task A but that has some correlation to it and some applicable insights. Perhaps another approach to solving a problem that is key to Task A, or a relevant issue that we hadn't identified before. In this case, it is best to "integrate" the useful aspects of Killer B into Task A, and therefore turn Killer B into Useful B, as illustrated below:

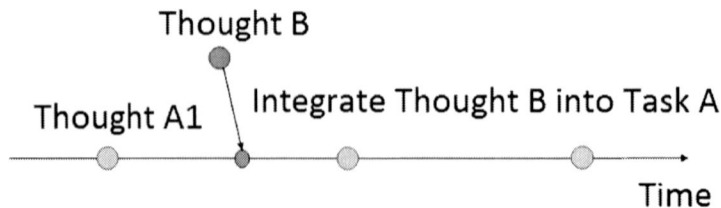

Thought B

Integrate Thought B into Task A

Thought A1

Time

Resisting Killer B

Sometimes, when we notice that we have been the victim of Killer B, and have been promoting Killer B or even actively contributing to its success at pulling us off Task A, we get into self-blame. The self-talk that we engage in can range from "I shouldn't be thinking about B right now" to the other extreme, which might be "I am a loser for thinking about B" or even "I will never get it right" and "I never get *anything* right," as our thinking grows increasingly irrational.

This is what we call "resisting" Killer B. Resisting Killer B is active—it's another form of promoting, and is just as harmful to our accomplishments. But resistance is a choice, and we can make another one. One way to do so is to reframe the resistance and reword the resisting thoughts. Instead of "I shouldn't be thinking about B," the alternative might be "I am glad that I noticed that I was thinking about B, and now that I did, I can get back to Task A." Reframing turns a problem into an opportunity.

How Do We Stay Focused?

Awareness alone is not enough to consistently keep us from running afoul of the thoughts that threaten our focus. We need more tangible and practical techniques to help us develop the ability to focus and cultivate "focus" as a habit.

First Technique: Using a timer

Not any timer – a countdown timer. Setting the countdown timer for 40 minutes (or whatever time period we choose) and then pushing the Start button has significant implications.

Just the fact that the timer is running seems to drastically heighten our awareness of time and allow us to quickly notice when we deviate from our task. It's as simple as that. It is fascinating that such a simple and easy tool can have such an impact on our focus, but it does. Buying a countdown timer may very well result in the biggest return on investment that we can ever achieve.

The Timer Creates Purpose

The timer helps us put a stake in the ground and declare that we have officially started the task at hand. Without such a clear signal it is easy to stay noncommittal, starting one task but then casually withdrawing from it to start another one. It is possible to keep testing task after task, escaping from the ones that are more difficult or less desirable, and sneaking into tasks that are easier (and, just as likely, less crucial) – I call this "task hopping!"

The timer puts an end to unproductive task hopping. It forces us to spend our time more purposefully on the task that we consciously select. This is a giant leap to become more purposeful. If you are thinking the timer is "just" another tool, and an expendable one at that, think again! The timer is revolutionary.

The Timer Creates Accountability

In addition to creating purpose, the timer also creates accountability. Now that the timer has started, in 40 minutes we are going to know clearly if we accomplished what we intended. The timer also helps us estimate time better in the future. Knowing how long it takes to accomplish any given project in such a time-crunched era is a rare and highly desirable skill.

The timer prompts us to move things forward

During the focused session, the timer improves the quality and efficiency of our work. It prompts us to face the issues, make decisions, and move things along as opposed to dwelling on issues and staying indefinitely in analysis/paralysis mode. In other words, the timer accelerates our pace and helps us equal or even beat the speed at which things are happening around us. What a competitive advantage that can be!

The timer as a stress relief mechanism

The timer signifies that we have given ourselves permission to be where we are for the time period we have chosen. Now we can more easily give up the guilt or anxiety that we would otherwise experience for not being somewhere else and not handling all the other things that need to be handled. With the timer, we are able to put everything else on hold because we have more "officially" chosen a path, and

---

most importantly a path based on purpose instead of a reactive one. The timer is the official seal of approval for our purposeful choice.

With the timer and the 40 minute sessions, instead of feeling guilty and anxious, we feel challenged to complete our carefully selected mission. Instead of taking on "life" and feeling overwhelmed and trapped, now we are taking on 40 minutes, and feeling hopeful. We are fully engaged and facing the issues for 40 minutes with a visible and bright light shining at the end of tunnel. What a relief!

The happy sound of accomplishment

The happy sound of accomplishment is only 40 minutes away, and when it is heard, we are likely to experience a range of thoughts and feelings, the most prevalent of which is likely to be satisfaction.

Stopping is critical at this juncture. Even a brief moment of acknowledgement goes a long way. This can take any form that is appropriate for the context. Sometimes a few minutes of letting our mind freely wander and allowing thoughts and feelings to surface can do the job. Sometimes this may require a more significant break and potentially some physical movement that gets us re-energized.

Which timer works best?

Any timer will do, but not all timers are equal. Timers that are software applications that can run on our computers are easy to find and many of them are free. However they tend to hide behind other applications on our busy computer desktops and therefore their role as a persistent reminder of time tends to diminish. Also, in a world of everything-electronic and everything-virtual, a physical item is likely to stand out and be noticed. In addition, an object that we can manipulate with our hands is likely to awaken and evoke motor skills that will add to the quality of our overall experience. All these factors considered, a physical countdown timer is best.

Second Technique: Micro-Planning™ each 40 minute session

Creating a brief outline at the beginning of each 40 minute session listing key steps that we need to get done in order to complete the selected task can make the session as successful as it can be, as illustrated in the example below:

Task	Update projections
Micro-Plan™	Download the latest spreadsheet
	Review the most recent guidelines
	Update the formulas accordingly
	Regenerate PivotTables and graphs
	Upload updated version
	Schedule meeting to review with team

Ideally the Micro-Plan™ is handwritten in just a minute or two in the Notes section in the paper journal that we will introduce in the next chapter. Alternatively you can create and use one designated Google Docs document that you dedicate for your Micro-Plans. In this case, I would recommend you add your latest Micro-Plan to the top of the document, following a blog-like approach where the most recent and usually most relevant information is always handy on top.

Just like the timer, which appears to be a simple and perhaps expendable tool on the surface, Micro-Planning™ is a powerful technique that can help us stay focused, and if and when we have to deviate to take care of urgent issues, the Micro-Plan™ helps us restart our task with the minimum amount of effort and the fastest recovery time.

As we get deeper into our task, the Micro-Plan™ can continue to evolve and serve as the short-term parking lot for new potential steps or related ideas that would otherwise derail us from the current steps. Our mind stays fully available for the core issues we are processing now. The Micro-Plan™ and the journal become our thinking pad and the extension of, and support system for, our short term memory, which tends to be challenged as information continues to relentlessly invade our mind space.

Micro-Planning™ and the timer work together to help achieve focus, purpose, and results that will add up to meaningful accomplishments.

Third Technique: Turning Off External Interruptions

It sounds simple, and it would be if all external interruptions were within our control. Wishful thinking!

Indeed, we can turn off the e-mail notifications, forward the phone to voice mail, and indicate that we are busy or "Focused" in our chat status, which we should do during our focus sessions. But it is much more difficult to switch off the people who stop by, the noise or conversations around our work area, and most importantly the urgent and critical requests that come from bosses, colleagues, customers, family and friends, not to mention the blame and guilt that come from not being available to handle all of the above promptly.

The answer to these external challenges is certainly not simple but it is an area where we have more influence than we tend to believe. To better manage these group-inflicted interruptions, it is imperative to a) find an agreed upon way in which we communicate to our team that we are focused (whether it is putting up a sign in our work area, or setting our chat status appropriately), and b) find an agreed upon way in which our team can escalate critical issues to us when such issues come up (whether it is cell phone, pager, or a special keyword in chat):

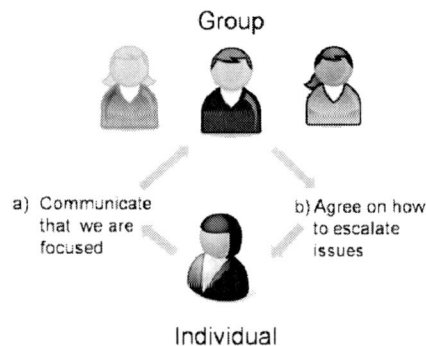

Group

a) Communicate that we are focused

b) Agree on how to escalate issues

Individual

The answer also lies in negotiating effectively with the world to help align goals and priorities and to optimize how responsibilities and tasks are divided and distributed. Using collaboration and information sharing technologies such as the Google Apps features we described in the previous chapter is essential in this effort and so is developing best practices around these technologies so they support us in this effort instead of hindering us.

In a way, this whole book is dedicated to acquiring the skills, and learning the methodology, that are essential for smart negotiating and for using technology effectively. To negotiate successfully, we need to have clarity, we need to have a purpose, and we need to have data, among other things. It is one thing to step into our boss's office and say, "I am overwhelmed and cannot get my work done." It is quite something else to show our boss a list of the competing priorities broken down into tasks and arranged in a timeline, with some initial thoughts on potential solutions that can serve as a catalyst for negotiation and for creative problem-solving (this is what the Immediate Priorities Matrix™ will introduce in a later chapter).

Google Apps to the rescue

In Chapter 1 we reviewed many of the key concepts and capabilities in Google Apps and one of them was the chat capability and the ability to seamlessly switch from one form or communication to another based on the issue at hand:

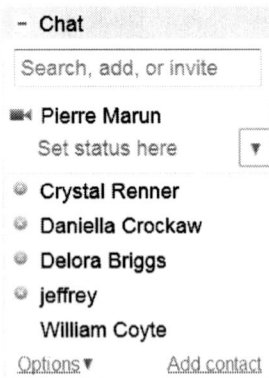

Chat allows you to add custom status messages. If you click on the arrow down next to the status indicator highlighted in the picture above, the following window will pop-up and allow you to create custom messages:

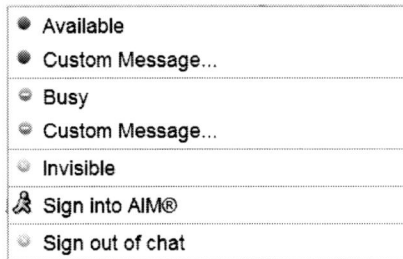

```
● Available
● Custom Message...
○ Busy
○ Custom Message...
○ Invisible
⅋ Sign into AIM®
○ Sign out of chat
```

Here are a few practical ways in which Chat can come to the rescue and help you and your team better manage focused and collaborative time:

a) Create a custom "busy" message and call it "Focused" and a custom "available" message and call it "Collaborative" instead of using the standard Busy and Available status messages which are less likely to get people's attention and more likely to be ignored.

b) As soon as you start your focused session, set your status to Focused, and as soon as you are done with your focused session, immediately set your status to Collaborative. Be careful not to leave your status on Focused for too long or keep it on Focused while you are actually collaborating. This would diminish the credibility of your status message and discourage others from paying attention to them.

c) Most importantly, inform your team about your approach, and even better, initiate a team discussion and agreement on the use of custom status messages. Such discussion will not be complete unless it addresses how to escalate critical and urgent issues that come up when someone is focused. The team needs to clarify and agree on what types of issues require escalation and what mechanism will be used for escalation.

In Summary

Let us move away from feeling hectic and head towards feeling calm. Let us move away from feeling overwhelmed and head towards feeling fulfilled. Let us move away from mediocrity and head towards accomplishment. Let us master the Accomplishment Zone™ and the Collaboration Zone™ and lead to a life of accomplishments. It is compelling. It is satisfying. It is yours, now.

Exercise 1: Managing Interruptions

List the main sources of interruptions in your work environment. Reflect on how much influence you have on each source, and what actions can you take to help minimize it.

Table 1: Managing Interruptions

Source	How much influence do I have over it?	What action will I take to eliminate it or minimize it so I can stay focused and reach the Accomplishment Zone™?

Exercise 2: Creating agreements

Reflect on ways in which you and your team can collaborate more effectively. Educate your team about the Results Curve™, Accomplishment Zone™, and Collaboration Zone™, and agree with them on how you want to communicate to each other when you are focused, and how you escalate issues when such issues come up.

Table 2: Creating agreements

Ideas for how to notify my group that I am focused	Ideas for defining what a critical issues is (the criteria that make an issue critical)	Ideas for how to escalate critical issues

Exercise 3: Micro-Planning™

Identify an important task that you would like to accomplish soon. Block time on your calendar to focus on this task (at least 40 minutes). At the beginning of this focused session, time yourself, and spend a few minutes putting together the Micro-Plan™ using the table below:

Table 3: Micro-Planning™

Steps	Comment/Description

Action Plan

Identify the action items that you would like to take as a result of what was covered in this chapter. Indicate the timeframe in which you plan on taking these actions. Then report on the actual date in which you implemented them and a brief note about the results.

Table 4: Action Plan

Practice/Technique	I will start implementing this on (date?)	Actual start date	Actual end date	Comment/Results
Working in focused sessions (40 minute, or your desired length)				
Using a timer				
Using Micro-Planning™				
Educating my team				
Agree with my team on how we communicate to each other when we are focused				
Agree with my team on defining what makes an issue critical				
Agree with my team on how to escalate issues				
Add your own item:				
Add your own item:				
Add your own item:				

Chapter 2: Meet Your New (Non-Digital) Assistant—simplify your life with the journal

Don't let the simplicity of the journal and how we are going to use it initially deceive you. Our workshop graduates incorporate the journal into their mix of tools and adapt it to fit their unique situation. It is fascinating to see what they have done with their journals.

If you're thinking "but I do everything electronically", especially that you have Google Apps at your disposal, you will soon discover the journal perfectly supplements the electronic world and plays an important role in helping us gain depth and perspective. The majority of this book is dedicated to electronic tools. But for now, hold on tight, and discover the journal! Later, you can decide if you want to use the journal as described here, or adapt some of these techniques and implement them in Google Docs--which we will explore in detail later in the book.

Today's Page

If you haven't yet gotten your hands on a journal, this is the time to do so. Open your journal to a blank page, write down today's date, and then below it, write down a brief outline of what you intend to accomplish today, as shown below (for now, and for the purpose of practicing, let us have one accomplishment, which is "Learn how to use the journal"):

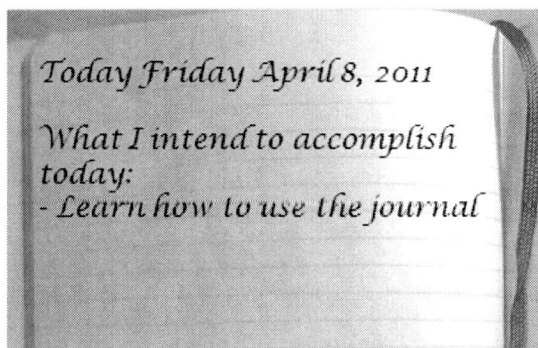

Today Friday April 8, 2011

What I intend to accomplish today:
- Learn how to use the journal

The Capture Page

On the next page, write the heading: Capture. This page is for to-do items and ideas that you encounter throughout the day, things you don't want to handle immediately but will instead capture and handle at a more convenient time.

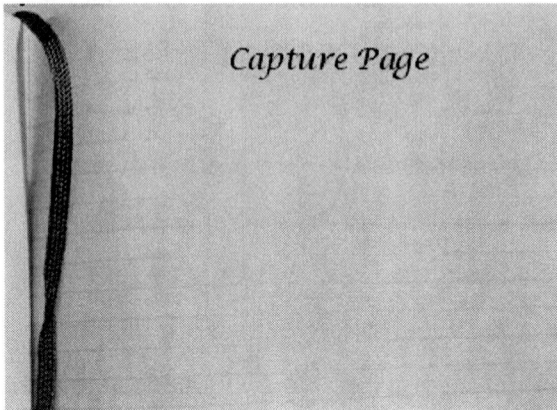

Capture Page

The Notes Page

And now flip to a new page and write down: Notes. This page is for meeting notes, phone conversion notes, thinking and strategizing notes.

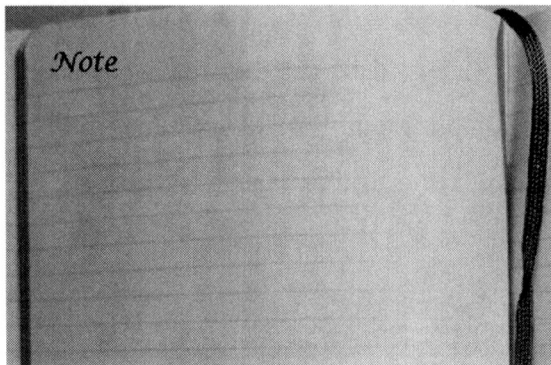

Note

When you're taking notes, and you happen to write down an item that you would like to act upon or follow-up on later, you may want to draw a little checkbox next to the item. Later when you review this page, the checkbox serves as a visual reminder for the action or follow-up. Then when you take the appropriate action or transfer the item to the to-do list or calendar, you can check it off.

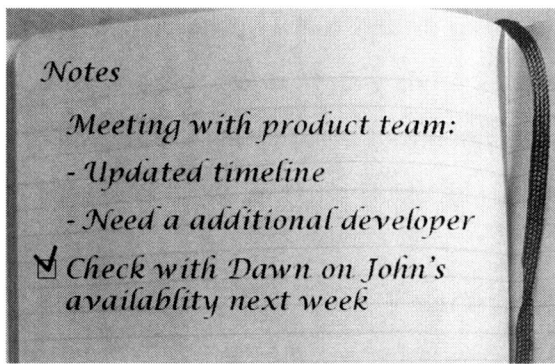

Notes

Meeting with product team:
- Updated timeline
- Need a additional developer
☑ *Check with Dawn on John's*
availablity next week

When writing notes, I recommend writing clearly and succinctly. It is more about capturing the essence rather than every single detail. It is about quality, not quantity. If you are a heavy note taker, I invite you to take fewer notes and stay connected with what is going on around you instead of being consumed by note taking. If you normally don't take any notes, and find yourself forgetting or missing certain parts of the conversation or important follow-up action items, you may want to start taking notes, capturing the key points and action items.

Writing legibly is also important, not only so that we will be able to read it more easily later, but it helps us slow down a bit and really notice what is going on around us. It enables us to write more thoughtfully, to write only what is important, and it sends the subconscious message to us and the people around us, that what we are writing is important.

One question that comes up sometimes in the workshop is why take notes on the journal when we can just use a laptop, or a PDA, or a smartphone? It is very tempting to do so, and it may be appropriate in some situations, such as if you are the designated minutes taker in a group meeting, or in some cultures where it is accepted and almost expected, such as Google. Otherwise, taking notes on a laptop or a PDA or a smartphone is likely to take your attention away from the more important non-verbal communication. You are likely to miss noticing body language where real communication takes place. It is also likely to be distracting to the other party as they miss your eye contact and your ongoing non-verbal feedback. In a way, it may cut short the benefits of the conversation.

Taking notes in the journal is less intrusive, usually much quieter, and much faster. You can jot down a few words in seconds, while your posture stays connected and engaged. You can resume eye contact, and not miss a beat of what is going on. This is more than note taking. This is preserving human connection and relationship building.

Finally, one practical side to the journal is that it can be with you at all times, it takes no time to get it out and open it, and it never runs out of battery.

Exercise: What are you hoping to accomplish?

Let us put the notes page to use right away. Take a minute to jot down the reasons why you are reading this book. In other words, what are the main challenges you face in getting organized, managing your to-do lists, managing your time, and reaching your goals? Maybe even list the areas in which you are experiencing stress.

I would like to remind you here about the technique that I introduced in the previous chapter: using a timer to focus yourself when working on certain tasks. Timing ourselves helps us stay focused on the issue at hand instead of letting our mind wander to unwanted territories. Timing ourselves also prompts us to move forward and make decisions instead of staying in analysis mode longer than necessary. Overall, it helps us apply our energy and sustain our attention to desired places. Start practicing the timing techniques now and give yourself one minute to finish the above exercise.

When we conduct this exercise in our workshop, we get a variety of answers including getting organized, feeling more in control, and managing competing priorities. We also get more specific answers relating to issues that participants are dealing with at the time, such as handling a difficult project task or issue, dealing with a difficult situation or a difficult person, or lacking motivation in a certain area.

Whatever you wrote down in your journal, it is likely that over the course of this book, you will find insights, concepts, and techniques that will help you tremendously in these areas, maybe even create a breakthrough. For now, we are going to put this to the side, and refer to it later in the book, especially when we formulate the action plan towards the end. Now you are ready to proceed with the next chapter, moving into yet another paper related topic – organizing the desk.

Action Plan

Identify the action items that you would like to take as a result of what was covered in this chapter. Indicate the timeframe in which you plan on taking these actions. Then report on the actual date in which you implemented them and a brief note about the results.

Table 1: Action Plan

Practice/Technique	I will start implementing this on (date?)	Actual start date	Actual end date	Comment/Results
Getting a journal				
Starting to use the journal on a daily basis				
Starting a new page for each day and listing what I intend to accomplish				
Starting the Capture Page for capturing items that you want to deal with later				
Starting the Notes page for notes, and using checkboxes to identify items that require action or follow-up				
Add your own item:				
Add your own item:				
Add your own item:				

Chapter 3: Mastering the Personal Zone—get paperwork under control

In this chapter we will cover some simple yet very powerful concepts that can help you organize your desk and are also applicable to the electronic world and to organization in general. Even if your desk is organized, or you don't deal much with papers, you will find the material covered in this chapter quite helpful and insightful.

Today's Page

Before we get started with the desk, let us first turn to a new page in the journal – a new day, a new page. Open your journal to a new page, and write down today's date, and then right below it, write down a brief outline of what you intend to accomplish today, as shown below:

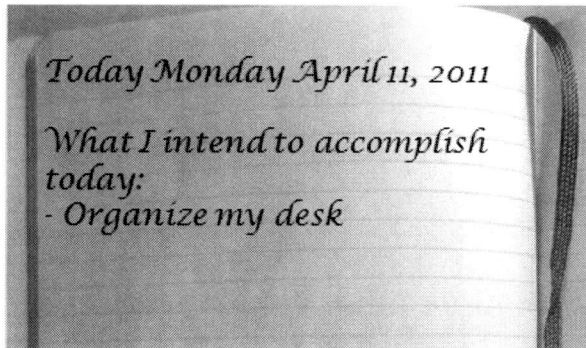

Then start the Capture page. As we explained in the journal chapter, use this page to jot down to-do items and ideas you encounter throughout the day that you don't want to handle immediately but rather capture and handle at a time when it is more convenient.

Capture Page

And finally, start the Notes page, where you capture meetings notes, phone conversation notes, thinking and strategizing notes.

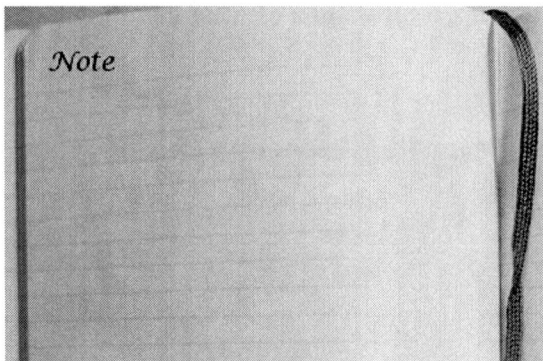

Note

As you read through this chapter, you can use the notes page to jot down key concepts we are covering and thoughts you have about the topic. Make use of the journal. This is your workspace.

Organizing the desk

Organizing the desk involves the demonstration of three techniques, one relating to loose papers and piles that we tend to have on and around our desk area, the second relating to reference material that may be scattered in our work area and that we refer to often, and the third relating to the inflow of papers and how we process them when they arrive to our workspace.

First Technique: The Work-In-Progress Unit

Why do we normally have scattered papers and piles of papers on and around our desk area?

Figure 4: Scattered papers on our desk

One reason is that we start to work on an item, but we get interrupted and move to another item. We leave the first item on our desk as a reminder, and with the hope that we will get back to it sooner than later. This happens again and again, and eventually our desk becomes full of these papers which we will refer to as work-in-progress papers.

To organize the work in progress papers, we are going to use a filing unit with hanging folders. This can be a filing drawer underneath the desk area or in a close by filing cabinet that is convenient. It can even be a portable filing unit. We will refer to this unit as the Work-In-Progress Unit.

Figure 5: Sample Work-In-Progress Unit

We will now gather the work-in-progress papers, not in any particular order – picking up each paper or set of papers that belong to the same issue or project, putting them in a paper folder, labeling it quickly by hand, and putting it in the Work-In-Progress Unit.

Figure 6: Related papers in a folder in the Work-In-Progress Unit

Then we take the next set of papers that relate to the next issue or project, and put them in yet another paper folder, hand label it quickly, and put it behind the previous folder in the Work-In-Progress Unit. Note that at this point, we are not concerned about ordering or prioritizing them.

Figure 7: Continuing the process one folder after another

We continue with the above process until all the loose papers are tucked in folders in the Work-In-Progress Unit. The benefit to this task is that we have transformed the scattered papers on our desk, which were difficult to work with, into small packets of information that are easy to go through to find desired information. However the more significant benefits of the Work-In-Progress Unit will become apparent now as we get into the details of how it is used on a daily basis.

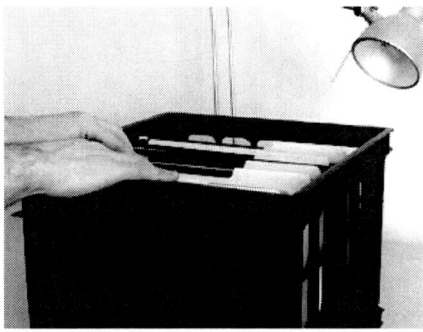

Figure 8: Scattered papers are now all in the Work-In-Progress Unit

The Work-In-Progress Unit in action

Now that we have our work-in-progress papers in the Work-In-Progress Unit, let's examine how we are going to use them on an on-going basis and reap the benefits.

Let us say I start working on a certain issue or project, and I realize that I need the related papers in the Work-In-Progress Unit. Therefore I go through the Work-In-Progress Unit, and find the necessary folder. Then I proceed with my work on this issue or project, making use of the papers in this folder as necessary. Now, let's say I am done with what I need to do for now, however, I am still not completely finished with this issue or project, and I am likely to refer to this folder again when I resume my work later.

What do I do with the folder for the time being? Obviously I would put it back in the Work-In-Progress Unit (after all, this folder still represents work that is in progress). The important question however is: "Where exactly do I put the folder in the Work-In-Progress Unit"? Do I put it in the same location where I got it from? That would be difficult to figure out knowing that the unit is not ordered alphabetically or in any predetermined sort order.

This brings us to the first concept I would like to cover relating to organizing the desk, which will also apply to the electronic world later: the most recently used goes on top. According to this concept, when I put the folder back in the Work-In-Progress Unit, I put it back in front of all the other folders—the most recently used goes on top.

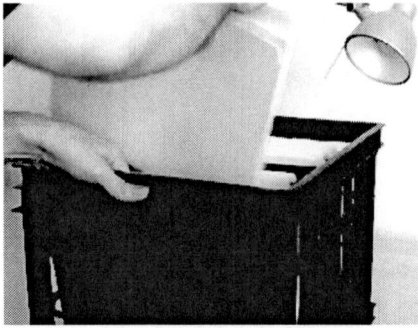

Figure 9: The most recently used folder goes in front

Let's take another example. In this case, I get a phone call related to an issue or project whose papers are also in a folder in the Work-In-Progress Unit. I quickly go through my work-in-progress folders, find the relevant folder, and pull it out. I then go through the papers within this folder and find the exact paper that I need for this conversation.

When I am done with my phone call, where should I put this paper?

The same concept applies. I put this paper on top within the folder, and then I put the folder back in the front of the Work-In-Progress Unit. So the "most recently used goes on top" concept applies even within each of the work-in-progress folders.

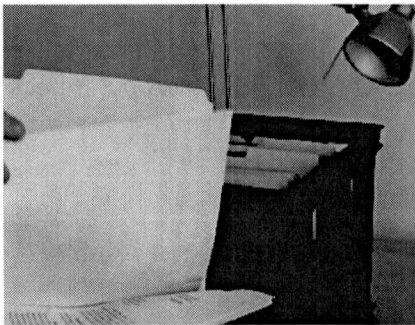

Figure 10: The most recently used goes on top even within the folder

As a result of the above, what will happen over time is that the folders that are in use continue to gravitate towards the front while the unused ones slowly but surely gravitate towards the back. In a few weeks or months, depending on your work cycle, you could take out a bunch of folders from the back, review each folder and identify whether the related issue or project is now finished. If finished, then the folder can be transferred to the filing cabinet, or otherwise recycled or shredded. If it is not finished, the folder is placed back in the Work-In-Progress Unit.

Out of sight out of mind?

But we are taking these papers out of sight, and isn't "out of sight is out of mind"? This is what some workshop participants say when we first talk about the Work-In-Progress Unit.

The out of sight out of mind concept is a misleading one as most participants end up realizing. First of all, when these papers are scattered on our desk, or in piles around our desk, they are no longer in sight. They are hiding each other and are often very difficult to go through. Second, even if these papers are well organized on our desk and not hiding each other, after a day or two, we get used to having them in sight, and we start to think of them as being part of the environment. They no longer serve as reminders. Therefore "in sight" does not necessarily mean "in mind."

"Out of sight out of mind" may work well if you have a few items to deal with, enough desk space to nicely spread them out, and if you are diligent at reviewing them and handling them in a timely manner. But once you have more than just a few items, without the luxury of a large desk space, and with the competing priorities and conflicting demands of today's information overload, the Work-In-Progress Unit will serve you better. When it comes to time sensitive items in the Work-In-Progress Unit, we recommend including specific reminders on the calendar or to-do list, which are discussed in upcoming chapters. Today's information overload requires a more structured and robust approach when it comes to tracking time sensitive items.

Second Technique: The Quick Reference Unit

The second technique relates to reference material that may be currently scattered in our work area. We are talking about information that doesn't change often and that doesn't require action. Examples are: Telephone lists, organizational charts, event schedules, product codes, just to mention a few. To help organize such reference material, I will introduce the Quick Reference Unit. This unit can be a vertical folder unit as shown below or a drawer in a filing cabinet that is easy to get to.

Figure 11: The Quick Reference Unit

Without having the Quick Reference Unit, this information would be scattered across our desk, pinned on our walls, or stored in electronic documents, just to mention a few places. The Quick Reference Unit consolidates this information in one place that is easy to reach.

Other examples of Quick Reference material would be project lists, maps and directions, and even articles or reading material that we would like to read when time allows. Next time we are going on a train ride or plane ride, we can grab the appropriate folders and slide them in our briefcase or bag.

Third Technique: The Inbox, Outbox, and Maybe Later Box

The third technique relates to the inbox, outbox, and Maybe Later Box shown below:

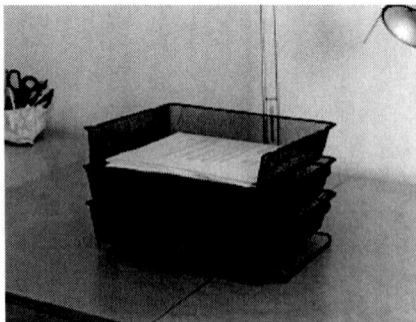

Figure 12: Inbox, outbox, Maybe Later Box

The inbox holds incoming papers that we haven't looked at yet, and that we still need to sort through. The outbox holds outgoing papers such as outgoing mail or documents that need to be distributed or handed over to others. If you don't deal with a lot of paper, you may not need a physical inbox and outbox. If this is the case, incoming and outgoing papers could just lie on your desk until they are handled. This may be okay if you handle these papers in a timely manner and if you don't have lots of them. Otherwise introducing the inbox and outbox in your work area may be helpful. Either way, it is the Maybe Later Box that is the most important here, and the focus of our discussion.

But what is the Maybe Later Box? The Maybe Later Box relates to creating space for papers that a) don't require further action (and therefore don't belong to our Work-In-Progress Unit), b) are not important enough to be filed in our filing cabinet (we don't want to spend time filing them and we don't want them to occupy precious filing space), but c) we are not yet willing to let go of them, thinking that it is conceivable that they may be of use in the future.

If we don't have a Maybe Later Box, these papers would take over our desk space, pile up around our desk area, and end up being the "noise" that hides the important papers and distracts us from what is relevant. The Maybe Later Box consolidates these papers in one place, keeps them out of our way, while having them still available for future reference if/when the need arises.

Occasionally you may find yourself referring to the Maybe Later Box, searching for a product brochure or vacation destination that you received a few weeks or months ago. It should be easy to find this paper by going through the Maybe Later Box where information is stored in reverse chronological order—with the most recent on top. When you find the desired paper, you can refer to it, take the necessary action and move it to the appropriate place. Then once or twice a year, you can take the papers that are older than three or six months and get rid of them.

Handling papers that come our way

Now that we have demonstrated the techniques, here is the summary diagram:

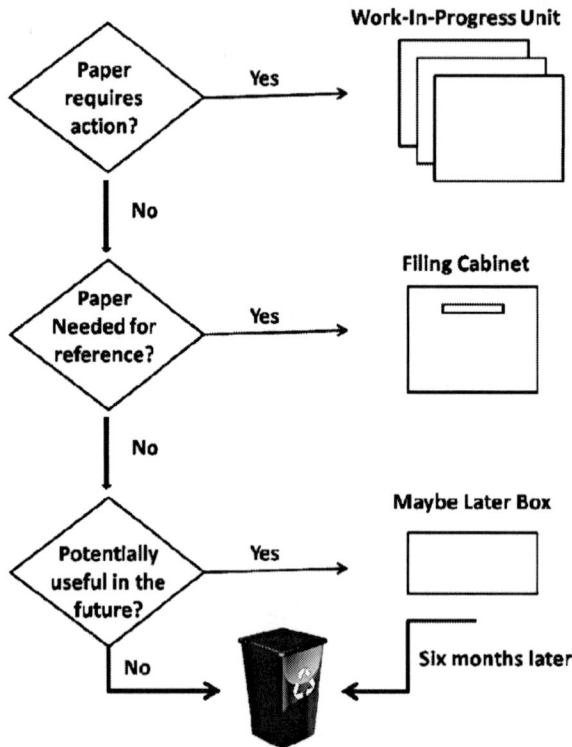

The concepts behind the techniques

First Concept: The most recently used goes on top

We already highlighted the first of three concepts that are behind the techniques we described earlier. The first concept was "the most recently used goes on top." This applies to the Work-In-Progress Unit and within each work-in-progress folder. We also used it in the Maybe Later Box. Let us now introduce and discuss the other two concepts.

Second Concept: Having designated holding areas

Each of the areas we discussed is actually a designated holding area. This includes the Work-In-Progress Unit, the Quick Reference Unit, the inbox, the outbox, the Maybe Later Box, and the to-be filed box if you choose to have one. What makes these areas designated holding areas is not only that they are designated physical spaces, but also that we have designated how we are going to use them and specifically which papers belong to which area. If we don't "have designated holding areas", out whole work area become one big designated holding area that is difficult to manage.

Third Concept: Creating distance

This implies distancing ourselves from information before we get too busy prematurely organizing it, prioritizing it, and acting on it. This is exactly what the Work-In-Progress Unit is about. This is also what the Maybe Later Box is about. These designated holding areas help us semi-organize information quickly and easily. They give us a chance to absorb what is going on and gain more experience with the information before we get too invested in it. In other words, they create necessary "distance."

In a world where information is coming at us in abundance at high speed, we need this "distance" to slow things down a bit. We need the "designated holding areas" to quickly and easily semi-organize information so it doesn't get out of control. We need to apply the "most recently used on top" rule to keep the most relevant information in front of us. The end result is that a) the noise is out of the way and the core information is easily accessible, b) we have more time to deal with the core issues instead of prematurely organizing, and c) most important we have better clarity and better perspective.

Implement as you please

Throughout this chapter, and the rest of the book, we present concepts and demonstrate specific techniques to show you how these concepts can be applied in your daily work life. Some participants implement the techniques exactly as demonstrated, while others tailor them, expand on them, or even re-invent them to fit their own needs and unique situations. We encourage you to experiment and adapt the techniques as you wish. The sky is the limit.

The Accomplishing More With Less Methodology, as you may have noticed already, is intended to be modular and flexible. It is not an "all or nothing" approach. There is plenty of room for you to customize. You can pick and choose the elements you need and adapt them to your environment. Then add additional ones later when the need arises.

The ultimate goal of the Accomplishing More With Less Methodology is to give you the foundation and the guidance to get started on this journey of accomplishment and self-fulfillment. How exactly you go about implementing it is all up to you!

Action Plan

Identify the action items that you would like to use as a result of what was covered in this chapter. Indicate the timeframe in which you plan on taking these actions. Then report on the actual date in which you implemented them and a brief note about the results.

Table 1: Action Plan

Practice/Technique	I will start implementing this on (date?)	Actual start date	Actual end date	Comment/Results
Designating space for the work-in-progress folders				
Designating space for quick-reference material				
Designating space for the maybe-later papers and material				
Having supplies ready (folders, pencils, etc.)				
Clearing the desk by moving papers to work-in-progress				
Add your own item:				
Add your own item:				
Add your own item:				

Chapter 4: E-mail Subdued—organize your e-mail inbox in no time

E-mail has become the obsession and addiction of today's digital age. In this chapter we will examine techniques to help us recover and regain control of our time and our priorities instead of being e-mail driven, and continuously pulled into different random directions (instead of staying focused and reaching the Accomplishment Zone™).

Today's pages

Before we get started with e-mail, let us turn to a new page in the journal – a new day, a new page. Write down today's date, and then below it, write down a brief outline of what we intend to accomplish today, as shown below:

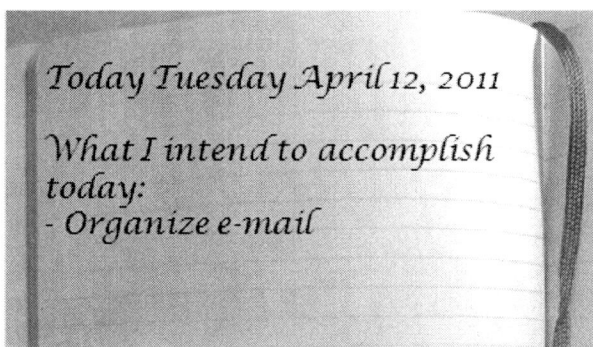

Start the Capture Page, and again use this page to jot down to-do items and ideas that you encounter throughout the day, that you don't want to handle immediately, but rather capture and handle at a time when it is more convenient.

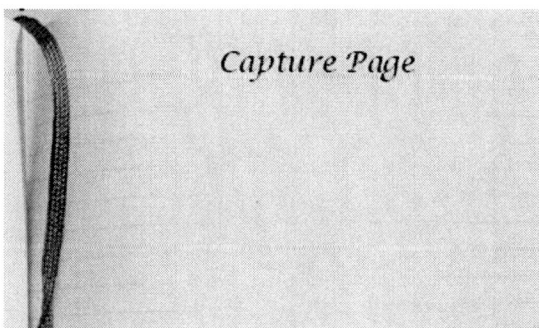

And finally, start the Notes Page, where you capture meetings notes, phone conversion notes, thinking and strategizing notes.

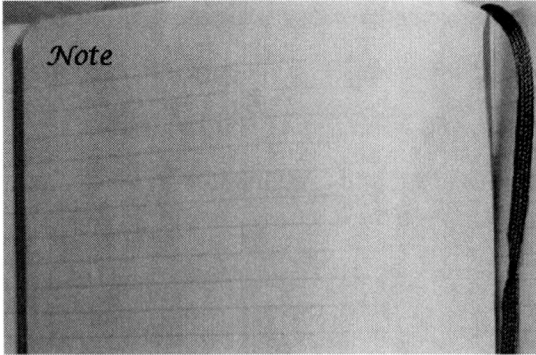

Adding Labels

Before we undertake this e-mail challenge, we need to prepare for it. This involves adding specific labels which will soon become instrumental to how you manage e-mail. Go to Settings in Gmail and add the following labels:

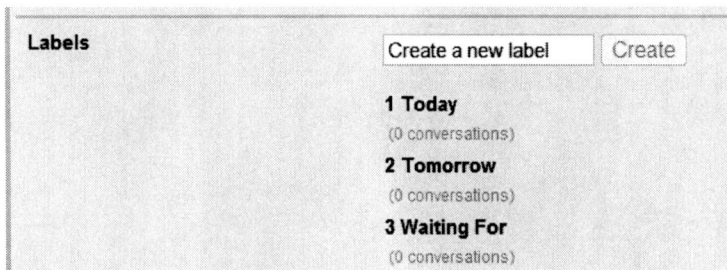

Figure 1: Recommended Gmail labels

Note that we included the numbers 1, 2, 3 in the labels so that these labels appear on top and in this order so we can easily find them and use them. I am going to refer to these three labels as "Workflow Labels" to differentiate them from the other labels which we might use for reference.

Here is how the labels will appear in your Gmail window:

Figure 2: Newly created labels appear on the left

Processing the inbox

I'm going to go through my inbox (from top to bottom) and examine each message and decide what to do about it--not only decide what to do about it, but actually do it before going to the next message. This is one of the fundamental rules that I suggest you follow consistently: Handle one message at a time, and one after the other without skipping messages.

If a message is urgent, or if it can be responded to quickly and easily, I respond to it and get it out of the way right away. Getting it out of the way might involve a) archiving it or b) moving it to the desired label for future reference. We have a lot more to say about archiving and labeling finished messages, but we will save it until later in this chapter. But for now, let us establish yet another fundamental rule: As soon as we finish handling a message, we get it out of the inbox either by archiving it or moving it to the desired label.

When I encounter a message that I cannot handle right away, I quickly decide when I am going to handle it, and then I label it using one of the Workflow Labels I created above ("1 Today," "2 Tomorrow," or "3 Waiting For"). For instance, let us consider the message from Delora which is shown below, and let us assume that this is a message that I cannot handle right way, but that I would like to handle later today. Therefore I select the message, and then click the Move To button and select the label "1 Today." The label clearly identifies this message as needing my attention sometime today and the message is moved out of the inbox and is now accessible via the label:

☐	**Delora, me** (3)	**Connectivity via internal Network** - I just got off
☐	**Daniella Crockaw** (2)	**Accepted: Strategy Update @ Tue Dec 14 1pm**
☐	**William, me, Daniella** (3)	**Getting ready** - Hello Pierre, Can you meet me he
☐	**Delora Briggs**	**The e-mail best practices document has been**
☐	**Chris Enly**	**You have been selected to take the Self Asse**

Figure 3: Messages in the inbox

Let us consider the second message in my inbox which is from Daniella and which I am not going to handle right away but I would like to get to it later today. However this message is time sensitive and I would like to get back to it in the early afternoon. In this case, it would help to have an automatic reminder. As we illustrated in the introduction chapter, this can be accomplished via a calendar event. And once I setup the reminder, I click the Move To button and select the label "1 Today."

And now my inbox looks like this:

☐	**William, me, Daniella** (3)	**Getting ready** - Hello Pierre, Can you meet me he
☐	**Delora Briggs**	**The e-mail best practices document has been**
☐	**Chris Enly**	**You have been selected to take the Self Asse**

Figure 4: Inbox after having labeled and archived the messages discussed above

Let us now proceed to the next message also from Daniella. This is a message that I will not handle right now, and that doesn't need to be handled today. I click the Move To button and select the label "2 Tomorrow." I am using this label to indicate that this message still requires a reply or an action of some sort, but that it can wait until tomorrow or the next few days.

Let us now continue with the message from Delora which relates to an issue that I would like to delegate to one of my team members. I forward a copy of the message to the intended team member adding my comments as necessary. What should I do then with the original message in my inbox?

If I am not interested in following-up on this issue, I can simply archive it or move it to the desired label if applicable. However, if I am interested in keeping an eye on this issue, and making sure that it has been closed, I might choose to assign to this message the "3 Waiting For" label.

Please note that I can also assign reminders to messages that I label as "2 Tomorrow" or "3 Waiting For" using the task list or calendar events. Please refer to chapter 1 for additional details.

Reviewing the labeled messages

Wouldn't be nice to be able to see all the messages that are due today, nicely organized in one place? This would obviously make it easy and efficient to review them and act on them in a timely manner.

If you click on the "1 Today" label on the right side of your Gmail screen, that is exactly what you will get:

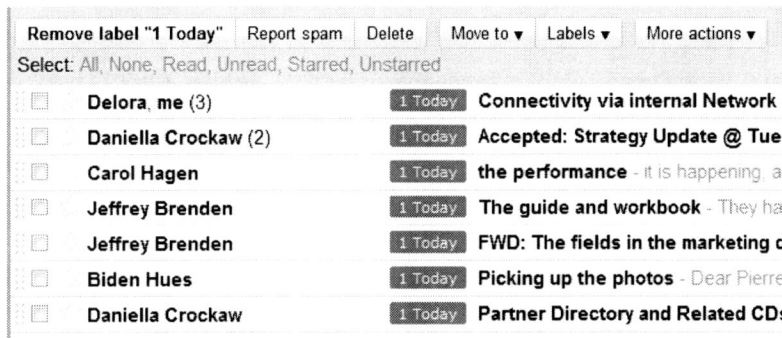

Remove label "1 Today"	Report spam	Delete	Move to ▾	Labels ▾	More actions ▾

Select: All, None, Read, Unread, Starred, Unstarred

☐	Delora, me (3)	1 Today Connectivity via internal Network
☐	Daniella Crockaw (2)	1 Today Accepted: Strategy Update @ Tue
☐	Carol Hagen	1 Today the performance - it is happening, a
☐	Jeffrey Brenden	1 Today The guide and workbook - They ha
☐	Jeffrey Brenden	1 Today FWD: The fields in the marketing d
☐	Biden Hues	1 Today Picking up the photos - Dear Pierre
☐	Daniella Crockaw	1 Today Partner Directory and Related CDs

Figure 5: The "1 Today" view

So what would you call this view? What descriptive name would you give it? Some participants like to call it the "e-mail to-do list" and rightfully so because it shows us clearly which e-mails need to be done today.

Similarly, clicking the "2 Tomorrow" label and "3 Waiting" For label provide a view of the messages that are due tomorrow and those that we are waiting for others to act on respectively.

Out of sight out of mind?

Are we taking these e-mails out of sight when we label them and therefore hiding them and forgetting about them? We discussed this objection earlier when we organized the Desk. Just as we indicated earlier, the out of sight out of mind belief is misleading. When all these messages are visible in the inbox, they are not exactly in sight, because you normally have to scroll down several pages to find them. The Workflow Labels allow us to get to these messages conveniently with one click. Having them all nicely organized in one view is very helpful so we can easily review them and act on them. Maybe it is time we put the "out of sight out of mind" belief out of mind once for all.

Archiving and Labeling Messages

When we discussed processing the inbox earlier, we indicated that once we handle a message, by taking the necessary action and replying to it, we move it immediately out of the inbox. We don't want finished messages to stay in the inbox and clutter it or hide new and important messages. Our job is not done until the message that we replied to is moved out of the inbox.

Gmail gives us two easy ways to get a message out of the inbox. One is to archive the message using the Archive button which basically moves it out of the inbox but keeps it accessible via search and also via the All-Mail label. Second is to move the message to the desired label. The latter assigns the label to the message and archives it all at once.

So when should we just archive and when should we label? Why do we even need to label messages at all? Why not just archive them all? Isn't Gmail the ultimate search machine and would allow us to find the information we need in split seconds? To answer these questions methodically let us consider the 80/20 rule.

The 80/20 Rule

If you work in sales, you may have heard that 80% of the revenues come from 20% of the customers. If you deal with technical support, you may have heard that 80% of the support issues come from 20% of the users. And there are many more examples. The one that I am interested in says: 80% of our results come from 20% of our effort. Yes, 80% of our results come from 20% of our effort.

80/20 Rule

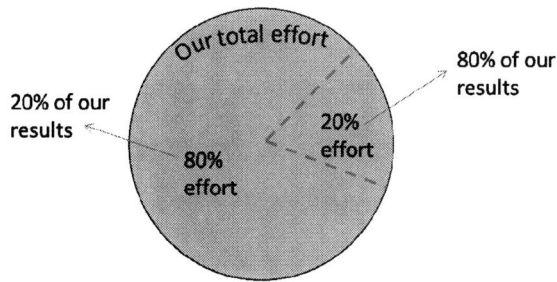

Figure 6: The 80/20 Rule

If you are surprised or think this is an exaggeration, do a little experiment. Keep a log of every task you engage in on a daily basis for several days. Then review the log and try to map it to the results that you are trying to accomplish. You are likely to be convinced. At any rate, the exact percentages are not the issue here. The main point is this: Most of what we accomplish comes from certain focused activities that we do and do well.

The 80/20 rule has many important implications. If we become more aware of this reality and apply strategic thinking to find out which of our activities creates most of our results, we can then do more of these activities and abandon other fruitless activities. If we increase the 20% to 30%, what do you think the total increase in our results will be?

80/20 Rule

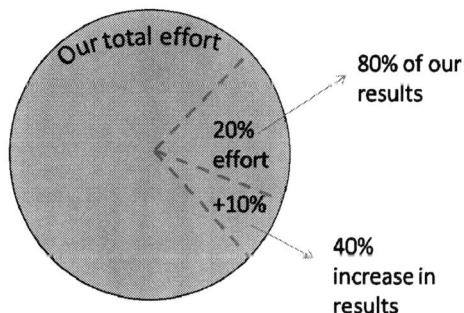

Figure 7: Increasing results

In fact, it would be about a 40% increase. This is a simple mathematical equation: 20% produces 80% of our results, so how much would 30% produce? It would produce 120% which is an extra 40%. So yes, a 10% increase in our core activities, would produce a 40% increase in the results. In other words, getting more accomplished is not about working harder and getting more done, it is about thinking strategically, and applying our time and resources in the most promising places.

The 80/20 Rule Applied to E-mail

So now let us apply this rule to e-mail. If 20% of our activities are likely to generate most of our results, we can extrapolate this to e-mail, and say that it is 20% of our e-mails that are generating most of our e-mail results. These are the core e-mails that relate to our core activities. The remaining 80% are likely to be more tactical and less important e-mails that don't have a significant impact on results. Back to the topic of archiving versus labeling e-mails, once I reply to a message, should I just archive it or take the time to label it?

If this message belongs to the 20% group of e-mail messages, I suggest labeling it and therefore having the appropriate set of labels to do so. For this to work well, we would need to have a well-designed set of labels that reflects a) our key business drivers, b) our key audiences, and c) our key subject matters. We will go through this in detail later in the book. Here is a sample set of:

Accounting
Administrative
Customers
Human Resources
Legal
Marketing
Marketing Online
Products
Prospects
Technology
Z-Personal
4 more ▼

Figure 8: Sample labels

If a message happens to belong to the 80% group of e-mail messages which don't have much impact on results, we don't want to spend the time and energy labeling it and having the appropriate label for it. This process can take significant time and energy. Instead, we want to quickly archive it.

Some participants ask why don't we just delete such messages when we are done with them? There is nothing wrong with deleting these messages. There are a few issues to consider though. First, you want to be informed about the retention and deletion policy of your organization to make sure you are conforming to it. This is recommended not only for deleting e-mails, but for managing other electronic and paper documents as well. Second, it is possible that some e-mails that appear now to be tactical and not too important, may become suddenly important in the future when related issues come up. Third, deleting can sometimes take up time. It is not the deleting itself, but the decision process that we might go through. If you find yourself questioning and hesitating as to whether you should delete the message or not, it is best to cut this short and just archive the message. After all, in the Gmail world, you have been given plenty of storage space and a great search capability!

Handling the Today, Tomorrow, and Waiting For Messages

One aspect we haven't addressed yet is handling the Today, Tomorrow, and Waiting For messages after you are finished with them. After you reply to one of these messages, if this message happens to be an important message for future reference (one of the top 20% that we discussed above), then you might move it to the appropriate label using the "Move to" button (see figure 8 above). For other messages, you would simply click "Remove label" to remove the label, in which case the message can be found in the All Mail label or using search.

Creating Filters in Gmail

Filters allow you to set search criteria and pre-defined actions that you would like to apply to the messages that fit the search criteria. To create filters, you select Settings, then Filters, and then "Create a new filter," and start by setting the search criteria:

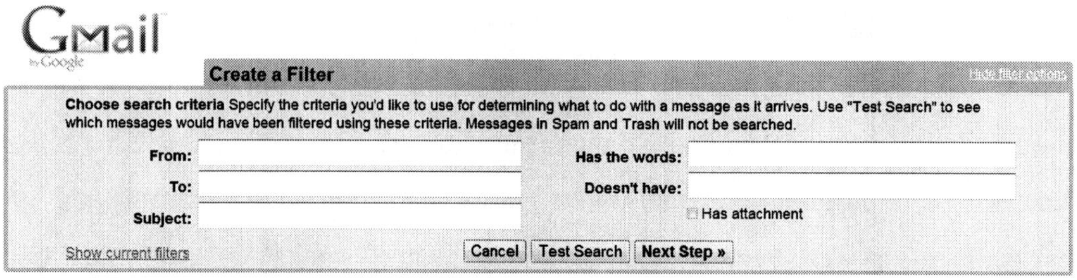

Figure 9: Creating a filter and choosing search criteria

Next you choose the actions that you would like to apply to the messages:

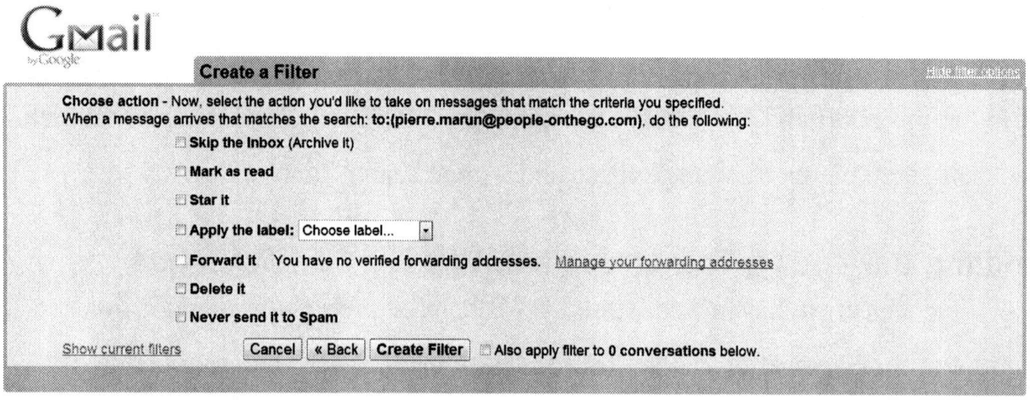

Figure 10: Creating a filter and choosing search criteria

Notice the checkbox "Also apply filter to the conversations below" which allows you to act on the current messages that fit the chosen criteria. Otherwise the filter will start to be applied to future messages.

Emptying your Gmail inbox?

"But what do I do with the 2000 messages that I have in my inbox right now?" ask some of our participants. If you have been using Gmail and haven't archived nor labeled messages in the past, you are likely to have thousands of messages in your inbox. How can you clear your inbox so that you are ready to apply the techniques described above? This process is actually easier than what you might think.

Here is the practical solution: Select a cut-off date that is a few weeks back. Then process the messages starting with the most recent and up to the selected cut-off date. In other words, ignore for now all messages that are older than the cut-off date. Once you are finished processing these messages, then create a filter in which the only criteria is the To field and in which you enter your own e-mail address such as:

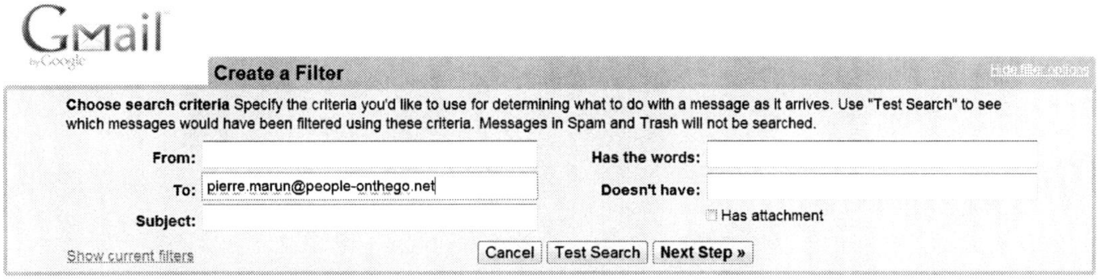

Figure 11: Creating a filter and choosing search criteria

And then choose the action "Skip the Inbox (Archive it)" and select the checkbox "Also apply filter to the conversations below":

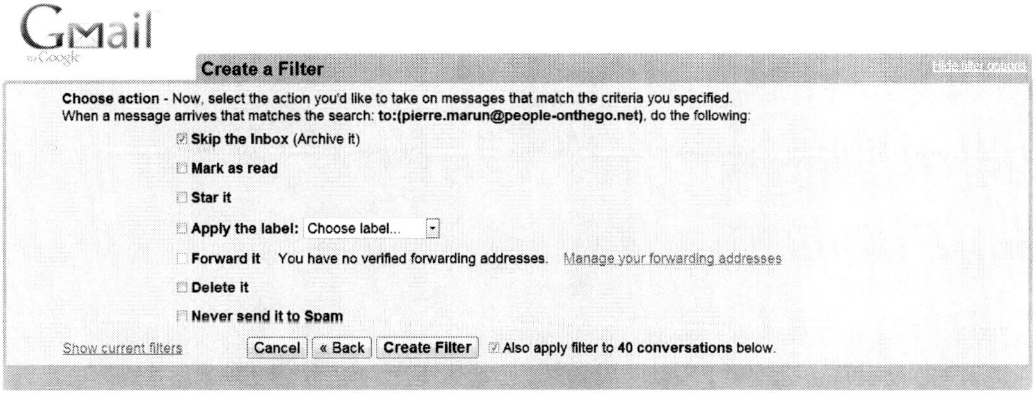

Figure 12: Creating a filter and choosing search criteria

As soon as you click Create Filter, the remaining messages in your inbox (all 2000 of them or whatever the number is) will be archived and now you have an empty inbox that looks like this (enjoy it while you can):

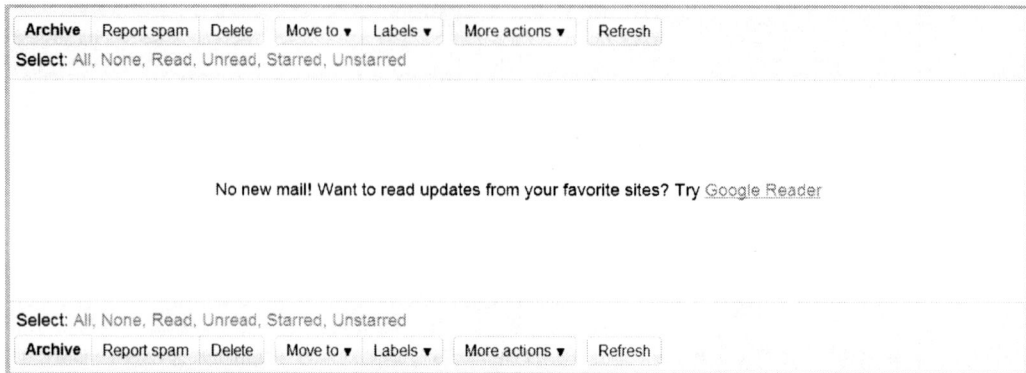

| Archive | Report spam | Delete | Move to ▾ | Labels ▾ | More actions ▾ | Refresh |

Select: All, None, Read, Unread, Starred, Unstarred

No new mail! Want to read updates from your favorite sites? Try Google Reader

Select: All, None, Read, Unread, Starred, Unstarred

| Archive | Report spam | Delete | Move to ▾ | Labels ▾ | More actions ▾ | Refresh |

Figure 13: Creating a filter and choosing search criteria

From ad-hoc and overwhelming to structured and manageable

Don't get me wrong. E-mail is still going to take time to process. As long as you have coworkers, friends, and colleagues out there in the world, and as long as you have an electronic mailbox, managing e-mail will continue to be a significant activity.

However, our goal is to transform this activity from being an ad-hoc and overwhelming one, to a more structured and manageable one. We want to make e-mail a repeatable task.

In this chapter, we built the foundation for better e-mail management, and in the next few chapters, we will complete the rest of the structure, and demonstrate how we can better integrate e-mail into the rest of our day, and make it not only a repeatable task, but also a contained task. Later in the book we will discuss how Google Apps can help teams and organizations share information and collaborate on projects and initiative while taking the load off of e-mail.

Our ultimate goal is not to let e-mail be out of control or even worse be in control. We don't want to allow anyone who happens to be on the internet derail our train of thought and take up our precious time. We want to get e-mail well under control and stay focused on what is important.

And now you are ready to proceed with the next chapter, moving into how best we can manage our workflow and get a better handle on our calendar, to-do lists, and outstanding e-mails.

Action Plan

Identify the action items that you would like to take as a result of what was covered in this chapter. Indicate the timeframe in which you plan on taking these actions. Then report on the actual date in which you implemented them and a brief note about the results.

Table 1: Action Plan

Practice/Technique	I will start implementing this on (date?)	Actual start date	Actual end date	Comment/Results
Creating the Today, Tomorrow, and Waiting For labels and using them				
Immediately archiving or moving messages after handling them				
Emptying the inbox using the filter described in this chapter				
Referring to the Today, Tomorrow, and Waiting For labels to see outstanding messages				
Add your own item:				
Add your own item:				
Add your own item:				

Chapter 5: Every Day Is A Complete Day—reconcile at the end of each day

In this chapter, I will introduce the end of day reconciliation process, which consists of three important activities that need to be handled at the end of the day. This doesn't have to be exactly at the end of the day, but as close to the end of the day as possible. Some users even prefer to do the end of day reconciliation in the mid to late afternoon because their end of day gets too hectic.

First End-of-Day Activity: Reconciling the labeled messages

As we established in the previous chapter, when we go through our e-mail inbox, the messages we cannot handle right away but need to be handled today, are assigned "1 Today" label. The first activity in the end of day reconciliation consists of addressing these messages. We click on the "1 Today" label to see all the messages that are due today, go through them and reply to them, taking the necessary actions along the way:

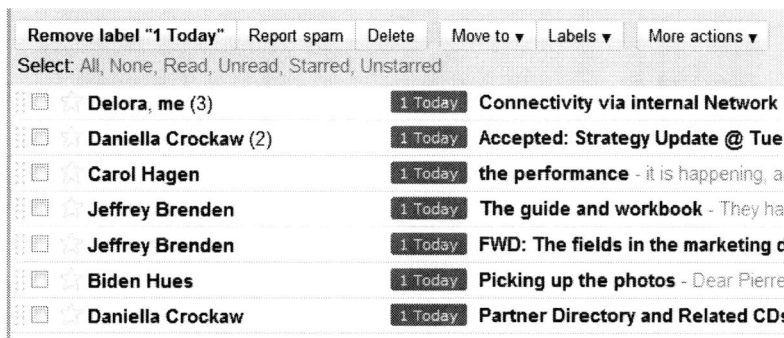

| Remove label "1 Today" | Report spam | Delete | Move to ▾ | Labels ▾ | More actions ▾ |

Select: All, None, Read, Unread, Starred, Unstarred

	Delora, me (3)	1 Today	Connectivity via internal Network
	Daniella Crockaw (2)	1 Today	Accepted: Strategy Update @ Tue
	Carol Hagen	1 Today	the performance - it is happening, ai
	Jeffrey Brenden	1 Today	The guide and workbook - They ha
	Jeffrey Brenden	1 Today	FWD: The fields in the marketing d
	Biden Hues	1 Today	Picking up the photos - Dear Pierre
	Daniella Crockaw	1 Today	Partner Directory and Related CDs

Figure 1: The "1 Today" view

The no-way-out attitude

Handling the above messages needs to be approached with the no-way-out attitude. Following the no-way-out attitude, you avoid any distractions, any excuses, and stay focused on this activity until you're done.

The no-way-out attitude is necessary because most of us tend to get lost in e-mail in so many ways. We get easily distracted as we go through e-mail. We think about peripherally related issues and our mind wanders to other areas. We take mental detours and even undertake other tangent activities, and as a result e-mail becomes a slow and inefficient activity.

In addition to distractions, we avoid facing difficult issues and making difficult decisions. We may be afraid to state our opinion, to be wrong or be held responsible, or to say no to people. As a result, we tend to gravitate towards the path of least resistance, and therefore handle the easy e-mail messages and leave the difficult ones till later, keeping them postponed indefinitely.

The end-of-day reconciliation and no-way-out attitude to the rescue

The fact that the end-of-day reconciliation is towards the end of the day (and that we have limited time left) helps prompt us to stay focused. Knowing that the end of day is in sight, and that we have something to look forward to, we are likely to stay motivated.

In addition, the no-way-out attitude helps us avoid putting off the difficult issues and making important decisions. When we face issues and make the decisions, fascinating things start to happen.

First, we gain self-confidence. We set an important precedence. Our mind learns that "if we are able to solve this issue, then we will be able to solve similar issues in the future." Second, we gain experience. We learn new information and potentially new skills which we can apply in the future. Third, we gain time. Instead of issues being held in our inboxes and slowing down our progress and the progress of our team, we release them and move projects and initiatives forward.

If you want to accomplish more in less time, less effort, and less stress, start by facing the issues. Not only you will save time and effort, but you will be able to capture windows of opportunities while they are open. Later in the book, we have a lot more to say about facing pending issues, but for now, let us proceed with the mechanics of the end of day reconciliation.

Second End-of-Day Activity: Reconciling today's calendar

What comes next in the end of day reconciliation process is the calendar. Let us consider this example of today's calendar:

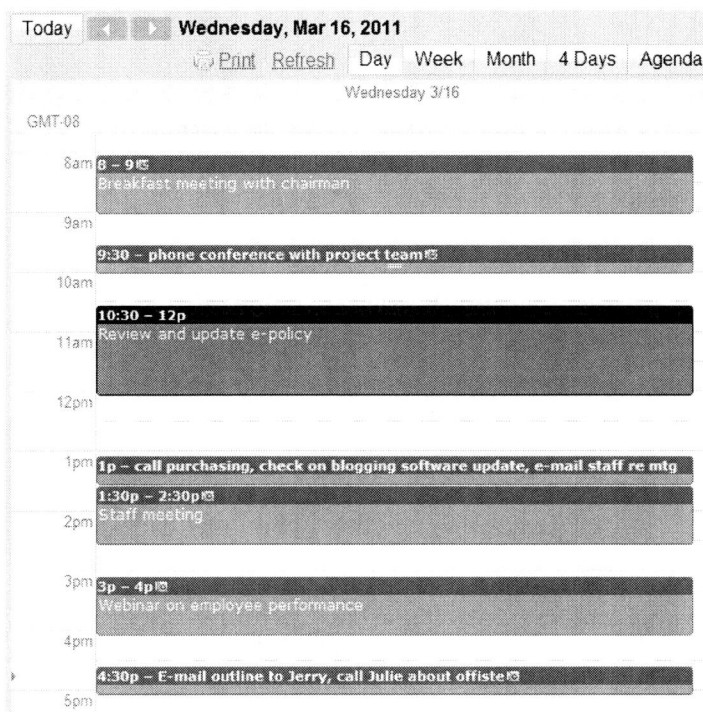

Figure 2: Today's Calendar

Before we start the reconciliation process, I would like to point out that this calendar uses color codes as follows (even though the colors are not apparent in the black and white picture above):

a) Red indicates that this appointment or meeting is fixed and cannot be easily changed—usually involving others or even initiated by others.

b) Blue indicates a time slot that we reserved for a certain task or activity—usually self-appointed and more flexible.

c) Yellow indicates follow-ups or other to-do items that we would like to take care of at the designated time.

Using colors was accomplished by creating three calendars, one for each purpose, and then assigning each calendar the corresponding color:

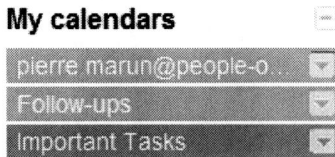

My calendars

pierre.marun@people-o...	▾
Follow-ups	▾
Important Tasks	▾

Figure 3: Multiple Google Calendars each assigned different purpose and different color

Reconciling the calendar consists of reviewing each item and determining if this item took place or not (in the case of a meeting), or if this item was completed or not (in the case of a task or follow-up). If the meeting did not take place, or the task or to-do item was not completed, then we need to decide what to do about it. This can involve rescheduling the meeting, or reserving time for the task at a later date, or updating someone about the status of the item, or some other action that is appropriate.

In other words, reconciling the calendar signifies closing the loops. Closing the loops is the foundation for success in the workplace and elsewhere. Without this process, we end up with chaos. Items may remain undone and fall through the cracks. Deadlines are missed and expectations are not met. A constant feeling of being out-of-control and falling behind tends to prevail.

Let us demonstrate the calendar reconciliation process in more detail. Obviously in this demonstration, we will be explaining the details of what we are doing and the underlying concepts, therefore this process is going to appear to be slow and time consuming. In reality, this process should take just a few minutes, sometimes a little longer depending on the complexity of the issues that you deal with. Most importantly, as you establish the end-of-day reconciliation as a daily routine, you will get better at it, and get it done in no time.

Calendar reconciliation demonstration

Let us start with the first item on the calendar, the breakfast meeting. I have had this breakfast meeting, so I am going to include a visual cue indicating that it took place by adding X next to it.

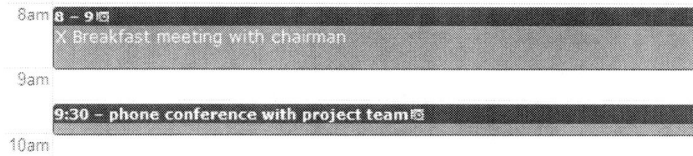

Figure 4: Breakfast meeting took place

Adding the visual cue is an optional step. You can alternatively just skip it and go to the next item on the calendar. However, the visual cue provides several benefits. When you look back at your calendar, for future reference, you will know with confidence that the item took place. Also during the reconciliation process, it helps you quickly see where you are, as you flip back and forth to other days on the calendar, or between the calendar and other applications. In addition, some users like it because it gives them the feeling of accomplishment, similar to crossing off items on a to-do list.

The phone conference also took place, so I am going to indicate so:

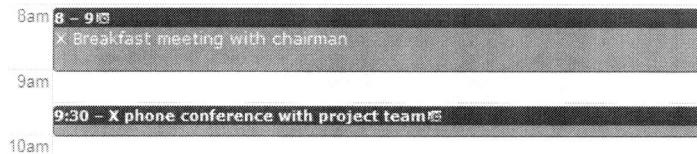

Figure 5: Conference call took place

The next item represents a task that I intended to accomplish during the designated time period: "Review and update e-policy project objectives and budget." While I started to work on this task, I did not complete it. I would like to find another time slot to finish this task, preferably tomorrow knowing that this task is due this week.

Looking at tomorrow's calendar, I find an afternoon time slot and reserve the time to complete the task:

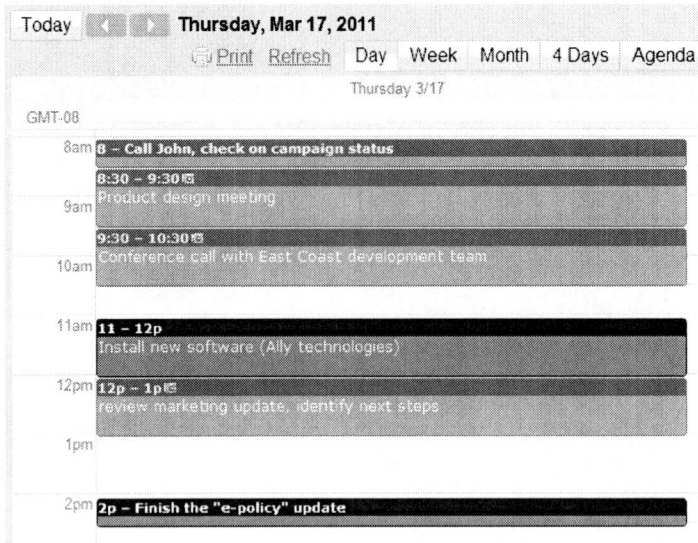

Figure 6: "Finish e-policy update" added to tomorrow's calendar

Now back to today's calendar, I would like to add a visual cue to the "Review and update e-policy project objectives and budget" task to indicate that this was reconciled. In this case, I might use a different visual cue (like X-WIP which stands for Work-In-Progress) to indicate that this task was reconciled but not completed yet:

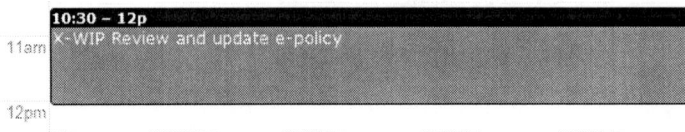

Figure 7: Item marked as reconciled and that in this case not completed

So, now it is going to get more interesting. I am at the next item which consists of "Call purchasing, check on blogging software update, e-mail staff regarding meeting."

As you can see, this item represents various follow-ups and to-do items that I intended to do. Let us take a look at them and follow the same logic as before, by adding the visual cue next to the ones that are done. I did call purchasing, so I will add X next to it:

Figure 8: Item marked as reconciled

Let us now consider the "check on blogging software update" item. This item has been on my calendar for several days, and even though I keep intending to do it, I find myself postponing it day after day. As a result, I am coming to the realization that for the time being, I have other more important priorities, and I won't be able to get this item done in the near future. Based on this realization, and knowing that this item is not time sensitive, I would like to "demote" it – take it off my calendar.

However, when demoting it, I don't want to completely forget about it, or have it hanging in the background of my mind, taking up precious "mind" space and energy. This is an opportunity to introduce one of the most valuable tools and important concepts which we call the catch-all to-do list.

The catch-all to-do list is intended to be a "parking lot" for the myriad of to-do items that come our way, which don't have a specific time frame associated with them. Instead of having these scattered on post-it-notes, or other paper or electronic formats, the idea is to consolidate them into one place in the catch-all to-do list. The catch-all to-do list can be in any format and reside in any medium that work best for you. It can be electronic or even a paper notepad if you wish.

Catch-all to-do list example

To illustrate the usefulness of the catch-all to-do list, we will use Google Docs to demonstrate this list. In this Google Docs document, I have a table of contents that includes some broad categories such as Actions, Calls and emails, Errands, Voice messages, Waiting for, Someday, and Ideas:

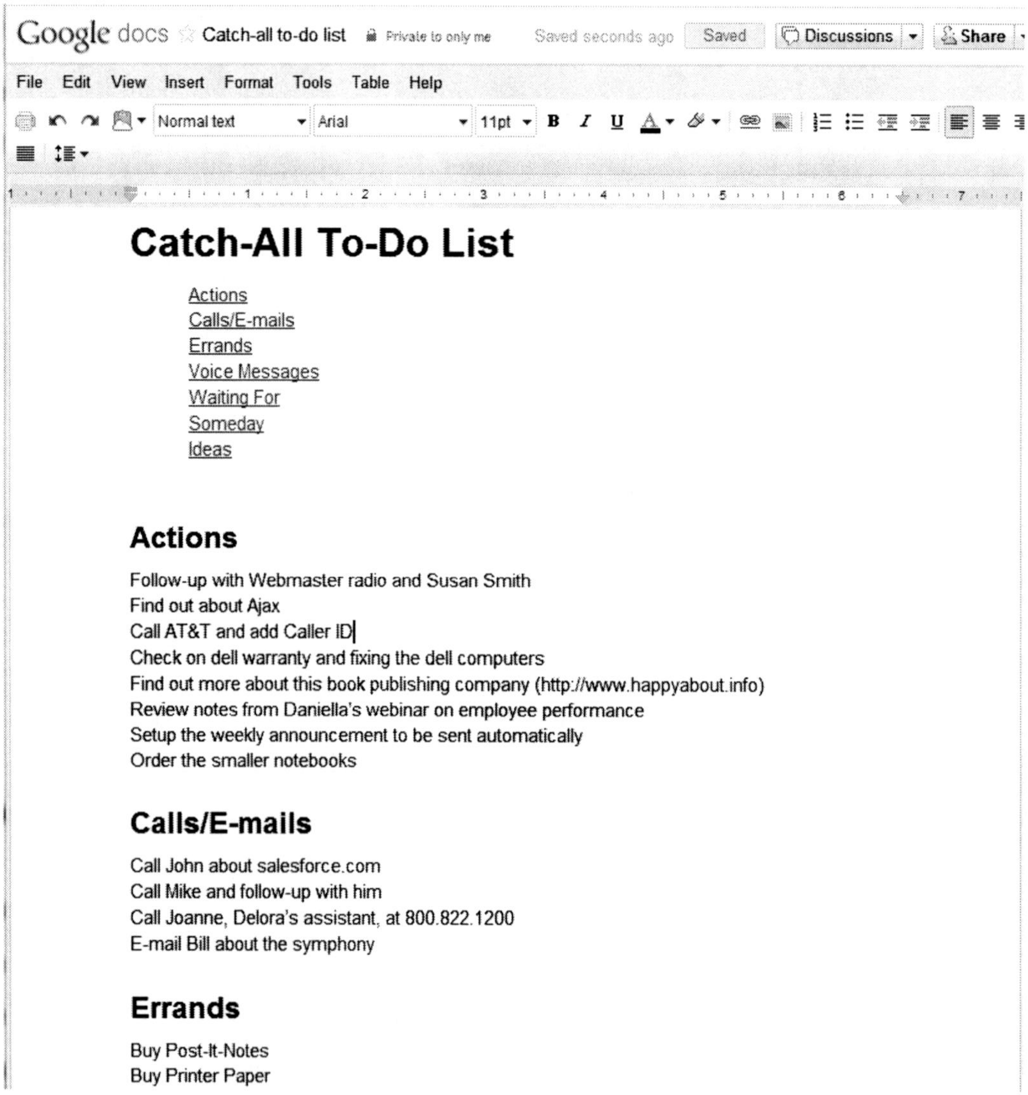

Figure 9: Catch-all to-do list using Google Docs document

This table of contents is clickable. If I want to see the Someday items, I click on the Someday item in the table of contents, and the following popup menu appears:

Catch-All To-Do List

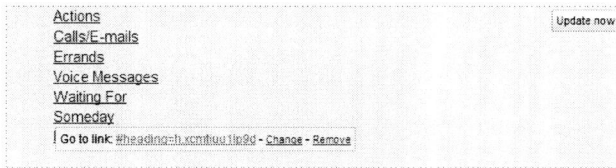

Actions
Calls/E-mails
Errands
Voice Messages
Waiting For
Someday

Update now

Go to link: #heading=h.xcmfiuu1lp9d - Change - Remove

Figure 10: Clickable table of content for each navigation

Now I can click on the link to go to the Someday section in the document. Later in the book, we will explore Google Docs' capabilities and demonstrate how table of contents work, and how they make the catch-all to-do list easy to navigate.

When adding items to the catch-all to-do list, I apply one of the concepts we introduced earlier in the book, which is "the most recently used goes on top." For instance, in the case of the "check on blogging software update" item, I first decide which category it belongs to, and then add it as the top item in the desired category. In this case, let us say this is a call that I need to make, so I add it to the Calls/E-mails category:

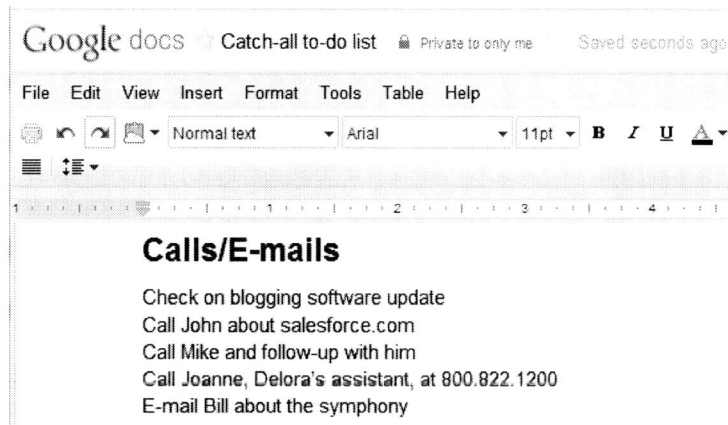

Google docs   Catch-all to-do list   🔒 Private to only me   Saved seconds ago

File   Edit   View   Insert   Format   Tools   Table   Help

Normal text   Arial   11pt   **B**   *I*   U   A

Calls/E-mails

Check on blogging software update
Call John about salesforce.com
Call Mike and follow-up with him
Call Joanne, Delora's assistant, at 800.822.1200
E-mail Bill about the symphony

Figure 11: Adding items to catch-all to-do list

The catch-all to-do list is a semi-ordered list

Remember the concept of distance that we introduced earlier in the book. According to that concept, we try to keep some distance between the time we are faced with information and the time we invest in organizing it. The catch-all to-do list subscribes to the "distance" concept very well. It is categorized which gives us some degree of easy navigation and access, but yet, within each category, items are not ordered. New items within each category are placed on top. This makes the catch-all to-do list efficient and allows us to manage large numbers of items without a substantial time investment into ordering and arranging those items.

Customizing your catch-all to-do list

The categories shown in the sample catch-all to-do list discussed above are probably useful for most of us. In addition, you are encouraged to add the categories that you need based on your work environment and preferences. The possibilities are endless and the sky is the limit. Below is an example of how one manager customized the catch-all to-do list to fit her needs.

Joanne happens to manage a group of five employees and has meetings with each of them periodically to discuss projects, performance goals, and administrative issues. During a typical day, Joanne encounters issues relating to her staff, or comes up with thoughts and ideas that needed to be discussed with them. Sometimes the issues are urgent and require immediate attention, but often the issues are not urgent and can be discussed the next time she happens to talk to them or meet with them.

Joanne created a category called staff in her catch-all to-do list and assigned it the Heading 2 format (like the rest of her categories), and within this category she created a sub-category for each employee and assigned to these the Heading 3 format:

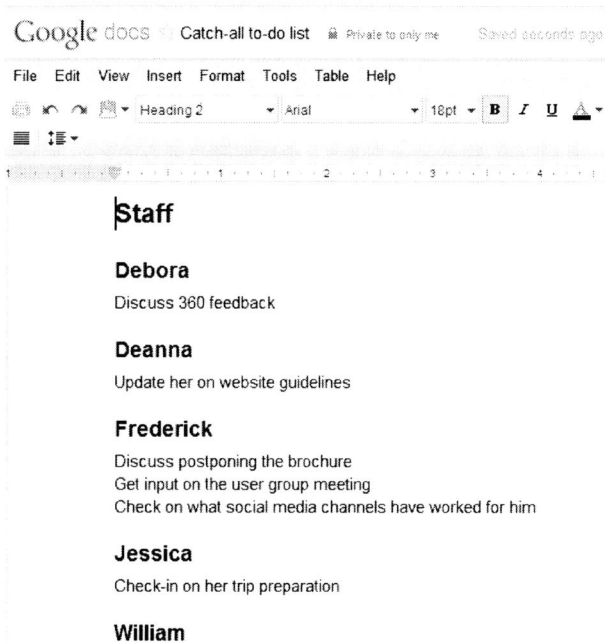

Figure 12: Staff category and sub-categories

When Joanne updates the table of contents of her Google Docs catch-all to-do list, the new categories and subcategories become part of the table of contents:

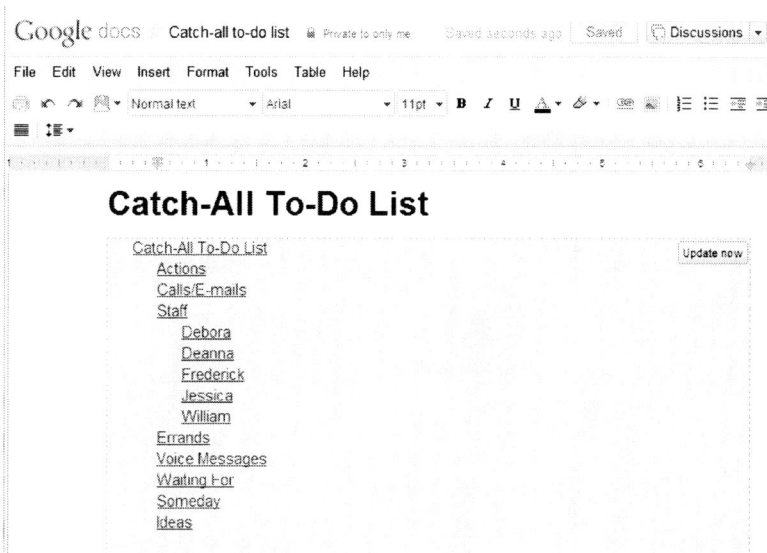

Figure 13: Updated table of contents

And now when she encounters an issue that she would like to discuss with Frederick for instance, she clicks on Fredrick in the clickable table of contents, and then adds the issue to Fredrick's list.

When Joanne has a one-on-one meeting with Fredrick, or if she happens to talk to him unexpectedly, she might go through the list with him. Joanne may even use the catch-all to-do list to quickly document the result of their discussion. This list also serves as a log for future reference, providing continuity from week to week.

Joanne's example is just one illustration of how the use of the catch-all to-do list can be broadened to help consolidate a variety of issues, easily and efficiently, without spending too much time organizing and prioritizing. After all, in today's information overload, we need to be selective on what we organize and prioritize. Our precious time needs to be focused on the key activities that are linked to our core results.

The general philosophy of the Accomplishing More With Less Methodology is that organization shouldn't become a task by itself. Organization should be "transparent"– a concept that we will keep coming back to throughout this book.

How long and how often?

The catch-all to-do list can get quite long. After all if you are a busy professional, you are likely to be bombarded by all kinds of issues that need to be captured. If you don't capture them in one consolidated area, they are likely to take over your desk, your computer, your wall, your floor, and your mind.

Philip saw his list become a very long document over time and he became concerned, thinking that he was falling behind. After discussing his concerns and reviewing his list in more detail, he came to the realization that the catch-all to-do list is not meant to be fully completed and concluded like a traditional to-do list.

Some of the issues which were captured ended up proving to be not as important as originally thought (the concept of distance) and didn't need to be done. In other cases, the requirements or scope of the project, or his responsibilities in certain areas, changed and the related items in the catch-all to-do list were no longer applicable.

Another concept that helped Philip feel more at ease with his long catch-all to-do list was the 80/20 rule. Philip realized that in reality, he could not possibly complete all the items in the catch-all to-do list. There was just not enough time. The only way to cope with that was to be selective and choose the activities that were going to have the highest impact on his results. This prompted Philip to do some more strategic thinking and focus his effort on these activities.

We can even take this discussion a step further and consider adding the Not-To-Do category to the catch-all to-do list, and then consciously move items that are not likely to have high impact on results to this category and therefore not do them. When you do this, you feel relieved and empowered. Saying no, not the casual "no" but the strategic "no," is one of the most effective ways to get more accomplished. Of course, in some cases, when you decide not to do an item, you may have some negotiation to do, and we will get to that when we talk about managing priorities and results in the upcoming chapters.

In conclusion, think of the catch-all to-do list as a choice list and not a traditional to-do list. It is intended to a) release your energy from being preoccupied by these un-captured or loosely captured tasks and to-do items, b) save you time so you are not prematurely organizing and prioritizing these items in traditional and time-consuming to-do lists, and c) give you an good overview of these items so you can act on them more strategically and decide what to do and what not to do.

The as-needed-basis concept

So how often do you review the catch-all to-do list? It is all up to you, and it depends on the types of items that you capture in the catch-all to-do list and on your personal preferences.

John decided to include in the catch-all to do list even short term items, and therefore review the list daily as part of his end-of-day reconciliation process. Christine includes only items that don't have a specific deadline or timeframe associated with them (as we suggested earlier), and therefore reviews the list once a week. Paul reviews the list less frequently and typically only on an as-needed-basis.

This as-needed-basis concept is yet another important concept in the Accomplishing More With Less Methodology. The methodology requires that you incorporate a few simple concepts such as the end of day reconciliation and the beginning of day reconciliation which we will discuss in the next chapter. The rest is all up to you and in most cases can be implemented on an as-needed-basis.

When you review the list, usually you will find yourself crossing off many items because they were already completed or because they are no longer applicable. You will also find yourself acting on certain items and getting them completed right away, or moving them to the calendar (i.e. promoting them) and therefore assigning to them a specific target completion date.

Back to calendar reconciliation

Now that we have "demoted" the "check on blogging software update" item to the catch-all to do list, this is how today's calendar looks like:

Figure 14: Item has been moved to the catch-all to-do list

The next item is the "email staff regarding meeting." I did not get a chance to e-mail the staff, so I am going to take a few minutes and get this done now, and then indicate that I have done it.

As you can see, the reconciling time is also action time. It is the time to finish some of the follow-up items that you wanted to do during the day but hadn't yet done. In reality, reconciliation time can be your most productive time. Once you get into it, you gain momentum, and become faster at processing these items and completing those that are still outstanding.

Now, moving to the remaining items on today's calendar, the staff meeting took place, so I'm going to cross that off. I was not able to attend the webinar on measuring employee performance, so I am going to reschedule it. Again, I might visit the webinar provider website now and reschedule it for another day, and then adjust my calendar accordingly. Finally, I am going to e-mail the outline to Jerry now, and then cross this item off. I didn't call Julie, and I prefer not to call her now, so I will move this item to tomorrow morning, adding it to the morning follow-ups, and taking it off of today's calendar. My calendar end of day reconciliation is now complete, and my calendar looks like this:

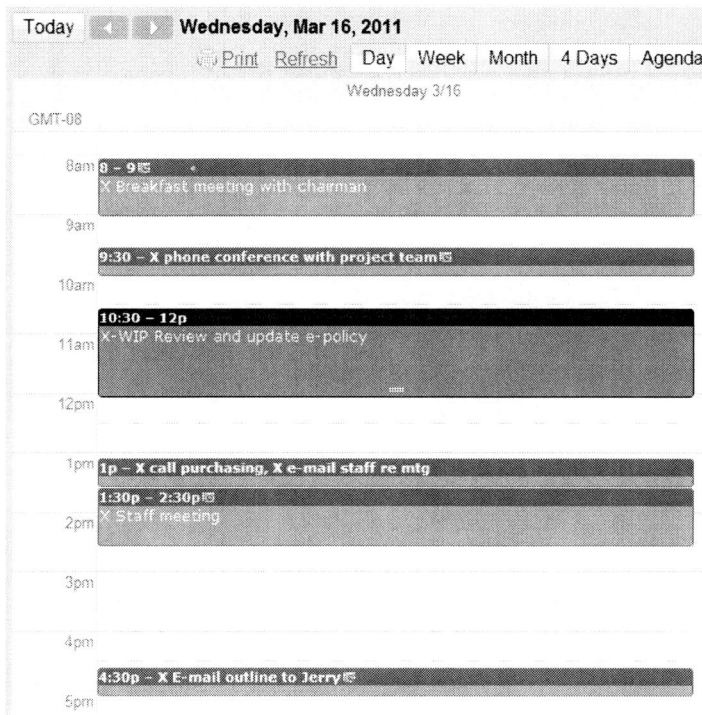

Figure 15: Today's calendar after reconciliation

Calendar reconciliation, a crucial awareness exercise

The calendar reconciliation process will end up being fast and efficient once you start implementing it and gain experience doing it.

This process has tremendous implications. Not only does it allow us to get many of our follow-up items completed, and make sure we are closing the loop on outstanding items, but it is also a crucial exercise in becoming more aware of how we spend our time and how long things really take. As a result, we get better at estimating tasks and also become more strategic in managing them, which are key factors for our success.

This process also acknowledges that we live in a very dynamic work environment, in which urgencies come up and priorities change. It is not likely that our daily activities match what we planned on our calendar. The calendar reconciliation help us account for these discrepancies by prompting us to complete some of the outstanding items and strategically reevaluate and reschedule other items.

If we resist this dynamic nature of today's work environment, we are likely to be stressed and jeopardize our success. If we surrender to it and use the calendar reconciliation to adapt and cope, we are likely to thrive. Imagine what would happen if we embrace and celebrate it and value the learning that comes with it!

Third End-of-Day Activity: Reconciling the journal

The third and final activity in the end-of-day reconciliation consists of reconciling the journal. What about the journal? Before we dive into reconciling the journal, a refresher on how we use the journal during the day might be in order.

At the beginning of each day, we start a new page in the journal. We reflect on what we "intend" to accomplish and jot down our intention for the day. Then on the next page, we reserve room to capture ideas and to-do items that didn't require immediate attention but that we want to track and process later. Then on the next page, we make room for notes. In the notes area, we capture meeting notes as well as reflect and strategize on things.

One of our workshop participants, spontaneously and with a lot of excitement, voiced a revelation she had as we discussed the journal, "so the journal is like an extension of our memory" she said. That is so true in so many ways. It is the extension of our short term memory. It gives our mind workspace to think, reflect, and strategize (the notes section). It is also the extension of our medium and long term memory, allowing us to capture ideas and to-do items which would otherwise be occupying and preoccupying our mind (the capture page). The journal is also a complete log of what happened which can be useful for future reference.

Most importantly, the journal serves as an extension of our memory by helping us declare what our intentions for the day are, and then serving as a reminder for these intentions throughout the day. The journal helps us put a stake in the ground as to what our intentions are, so we don't continue to escape them or avoid them, as our mind comes up with clever excuses, and derails us into the path of least resistance.

Let us now get into the journal reconciliation.

Reconciling Today's Page in the Journal

We will review what we intended to accomplish today, and schedule outstanding items on our calendar or occasionally capture them in the catch-all to-do list. This is also the time to feel proud of what we have accomplished. There is always so much more to be done that we normally forget to stop and appreciate what we have completed.

This is what today's intentions page might look like when reconciled:

Figure 16: Today's page in the journal after reconciliation

Note that we used a visual cue similar to the one we used in calendar to indicate that an item has been completed. We also used a new notation ">" to indicate that an item has been rescheduled or moved to the catch all to-do list.

Reconciling the Capture Page in the Journal

Then we need to go through the Capture Page, review the items on this page and reconcile them. This may also be a good time to get some of these items done. Jennifer captured the following items on her Capture Page in the calendar:

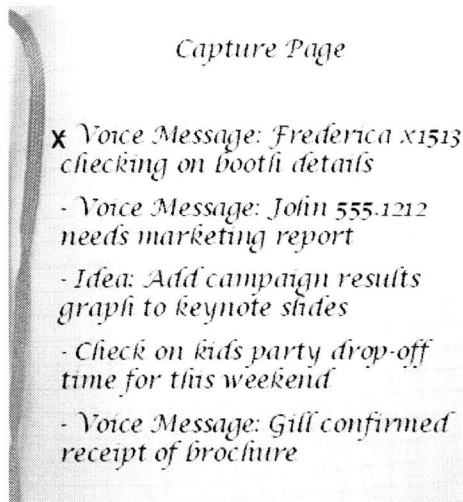

Capture Page

x *Voice Message: Frederica x1513 checking on booth details*

- *Voice Message: John 555.1212 needs marketing report*

- *Idea: Add campaign results graph to keynote slides*

- *Check on kids party drop-off time for this weekend*

- *Voice Message: Gill confirmed receipt of brochure*

Figure 17: Capture page in the journal before reconciliation

Notice the "X" next to the first voice message from Frederica. This signifies that she already took care of this item. During the journal reconciliation, Jennifer manages to complete many of these items and move others to the calendar or the catch-all to-do list as follows.

First she e-mails John the marketing report. She captures 'add campaign results to slides' in the ideas section of her catch-all to-do list. She sends a text message to her friend asking about the drop-off time for this weekend. And then, she e-mails Gill the next shipment information.

Here is her Capture page now:

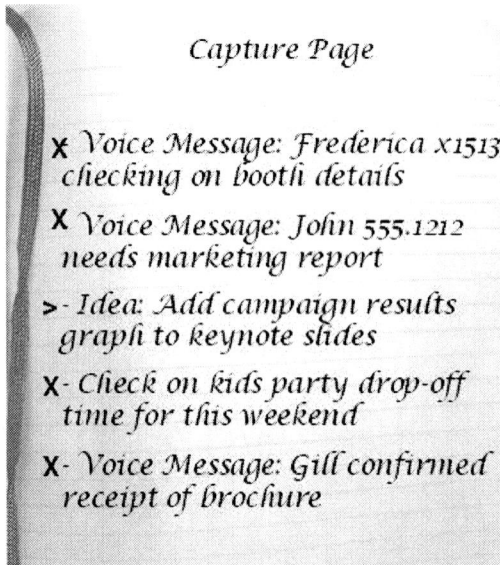

Capture Page

x *Voice Message: Frederica x1513 checking on booth details*

x *Voice Message: John 555.1212 needs marketing report*

> *Idea: Add campaign results graph to keynote slides*

x *Check on kids party drop-off time for this weekend*

x *Voice Message: Gill confirmed receipt of brochure*

Figure 18: Capture Page in the journal after reconciliation

There is a lot to learn from Jennifer's way of handling her Capture Page. First Jennifer uses this page not only to capture potential to-do items and ideas, but also voice messages. Capturing voice messages on this page helped her easily identify them at a glance and manage them in one place instead of having them scattered on post-it notes and papers around her desk. She can track which ones have been dealt with and which ones are outstanding, and have a log of them with the corresponding details such as telephone numbers and issues for future reference.

Note that Jennifer tracked ideas that came to her mind throughout the day by jotting them down on the Capture Page as well. When do new ideas and creative thoughts come to us? Do they come to us when we sit down and request that they do? Not usually. Our mind seems to somehow shoot them out at the least expected times and in the least favorable circumstances. If we don't capture them, they will continue to preoccupy our mind, and in some cases they can be forgotten and un-utilized. The Capture Page provides the opportunity to capture these ideas. Additionally, the catch-all to do list allows us to park them until they can be leveraged.

As you can see, the journal can be your companion throughout the day. Depending on your preference, and how large your briefcase or purse is, your journal can be the regular 8.5" x 11" size, or the 5.25" x 8.25" size, like one of the popular Moleskine journals, or even the smaller 3.5" x 5.5" pocketsize notebook, which is another popular Moleskine journal. One journal brand that is also popular is the Levenger journal where pages can be easily added and taken out. Some of our workshop participants find numerous advantages and applications for this feature and come up with new and interesting ways of using their Levenger journals.

Paper or electronic? What is the answer?

During our workshops, we often get into a discussion about why we should use a paper journal in a world that seems to be run by electronic tools. Below are some notes about the advantages of the paper journal, but if you believe that you can accomplish the same purposes electronically, then you may not need the paper journal.

Advantages of the paper journal

In my experience, and the experience of many of our workshop participants, the paper journal offers three advantages over electronic tools: Speed, portability, and perspective. It takes just a few seconds, literally 5 to 10 seconds, to capture an important note in the paper journal. In the electronic world, this may take much longer especially if you are dealing with a small keyboard on a mobile device.

More often than not, we don't have much time, and most often, we get these great ideas or get reminded about these to-do items or issues in the middle of in-person meetings, during phone conferences, or while we are in transition. Every second counts. This is especially true when we are communicating with other people and don't want to eye contact for too long. These are the times where laptops and smartphones can get in the way. A paper journal is much "quieter", less intrusive, and less demanding.

While portability of electronic gear has come a long way, and continues to with the ongoing introductions of light and thin products, it will be a long time before it can compete with the paper journal which has taken portability to a whole new level. For one thing, the paper journal weighs very little, does not require any accessories, and never runs out of battery.

The most important and strategic advantage of the paper journal is perspective. We are so immersed in the electronic world that we often end up losing perspective. The journal rescues us from drowning in the ocean of electronic information, and encourages us to stay in touch with what is happening around us. It helps us focus on what is important. In addition, freely drawing in our notes page as we think and strategize about important issues can help us unleash our creativity and problem solving skills.

In conclusion, we find the paper journal to be a great complement to the electronic tools that we use every day. It provides additional speed, portability, and perspective. It supports our information capture needs as well as serves as a playground for our creative thinking and strategizing. I recommend you find out which journal works best for you, experiment with it, and tailor your use based on your needs and preferences.

Reconciling the Notes Pages

Remember the tip I mentioned very early in the book about note taking? I suggested that you add a checkbox (an empty square) in the left margin next to action items and items that require a follow-up of some sort. These checkboxes pay off now during the reconciliation process.

Reconciling the notes pages consists of skimming these pages quickly and looking for these checkboxes. When you find a checkbox, you can reconcile the item by taking the action now, scheduling it for later, or capturing it on the catch-all to do list. Jerry found two checkboxes today, relating to meetings he attended and managed to take the necessary actions and check them off:

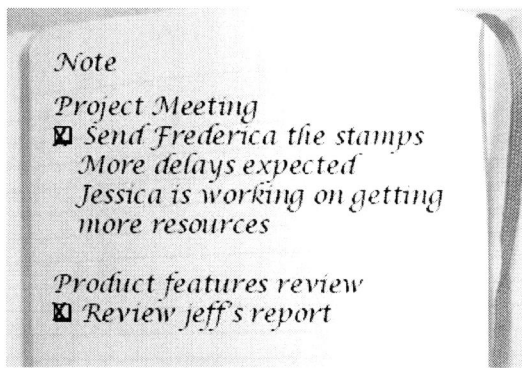

Figure 19: Journal Notes Page after reconciliation

Back to the concept of distance

The journal enables us to capture information when we are faced with it, and then process it later, mainly during the end-of-day reconciliation. This is the perfect example of the concept of distance that was presented earlier in the book. Instead of taking too much time and energy trying to figure out the importance of this information and what to do about it, we let it rest a bit, and give ourselves a chance to gain some perspective.

During the end-of-day reconciliation, we may decide that this action item or idea is not as important or as promising as it appeared when we were first faced with it. We may then transfer it to the catch-all to-do list for the future reference or even cross it off permanently. When this happens, and it is likely to happen often enough, you will be happy that you didn't invest too much time and energy in this item in the first place.

How about journaling

It is a journal after all. If you are inclined to journal, or want to give this technique a try, the journal is the ideal place to do it. This can be a practice that you do on a regular basis or on an as-needed basis. Journaling about lessoned learned for example can be a powerful way to leverage them in the future. We somehow seem to skip over important lessons learned as they stay afloat in our mind and then somehow disappear. Journaling can help crystallize our learning. Journaling also helps affirm an intention to apply the learning in the future. There is a strong relationship between clear intentions and future actions. Journaling can strengthen the link between the two.

Let us take the journaling practice into yet another level. Do you want to make a change in your life but don't know where to start or still hesitating or lacking motivation? Try journaling about it on a daily basis for a week or two. Then leave it alone and see what happens. At least, you gain more clarity on the situation. At best, your commitment level increases and you find yourself taking concrete actions.

Sometimes, to your surprise, after journaling about a desired change or goal, you may come to the conclusion that it isn't really what you want or not as important as you thought. You can then more peacefully let go of it instead of continuing to hold on to it.

Dare to journal! The results can be beyond your imagination.

Tracking to do items that have deadlines

During the reconciliation process, we used the catch-all to-do list to capture items that don't have a specific deadline or desired timeframe associated with them. How about those items that have a deadline or a desired timeframe? Where would we track these?

As Monique was reconciling her Capture Page in the journal, she encountered the following two items which she took note of during the day:

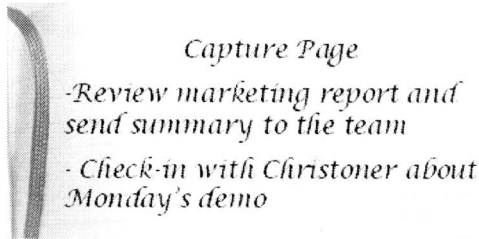

Capture Page
-Review marketing report and send summary to the team
- Check-in with Christoner about Monday's demo

Figure 20: Capture Page items to be reconciled

Reviewing the marketing report needs to be accomplished by end of day tomorrow. Monique reserves 30 minute on her calendar to review the report and send the summary to her team. Checking-in with Christopher involves a quick e-mail or phone call, and is not likely to take more than just a few minutes. Monique included this also on her calendar together with a number of other follow-ups that she already had scheduled for the early afternoon:

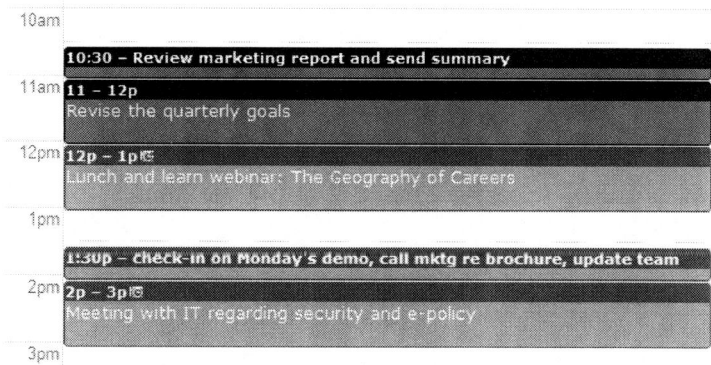

Figure 21: Capture Page items reconciled and moved to tomorrow's calendar

As you can see Monique is tracking to-do items that have a deadline or a desired timeframe on her calendar. John, another participant, decided to track such

---

items in Tasks in Google Apps and assign a due date to each task (clicking Tasks in the left panel in Gmail displays the task list on the right hand side so it stays visible). While Susan opted to have a running list on a separate paper notepad dedicated to these items.

For John and for Susan, the end-of-day reconciliation process should be expanded to include their to-do lists, which we refer to as short-term to-do list to differentiate them from the catch-all to-so list. This would involve reviewing the short term to-do list, crossing off completed items, potentially adjusting the priority and due date for other items, and adding more items as necessary.

Whether you keep such items on your Calendar, similar to what Monique did, or on a separate short-term to-do list, similar to what John and Susan did, is mostly a personal preference. What is important is to make sure that this list is included in the reconciliation process and well integrated with the rest of your system. It is also important to note that this list is substantially different from the catch-all to-do list and serves a different purpose. The two complement each other quite well.

If I was to recommend an approach, I would recommend Monique's approach for the following reasons. First, for to-do items that are going to take up a chunk of our time, like reviewing the report in Monique's case, having such items on our calendar helps us reserve time for them instead of allowing our calendar to be filled up with back to back meetings for instance. This technique also give us a better visual indication of how busy we are and how committed our time is, so we can easily determine how much more we can take on, and better estimate when we can get things done. In addition, it helps us solidify our intention of getting the item completed in the desired timeframe.

Having the less significant follow-up items on our calendar, such as checking-in with Christopher regarding Monday's demo, not only saves us the time of repeatedly scanning a separate to-do list, but also brings such items to the foreground, and serves as a non-intrusive reminder for these items as we review our calendar during the day.

End-of-day reconciliation in review

The reconciliation process as outlined above included three important parts:

1) Processing Today's e-mail messages that were labeled for today

2) Reviewing today's calendar items, marking off those that were completed, and completing or rearranging those that are still outstanding

3) Reviewing today's journal pages, and completing or rearranging those items that are still outstanding

Our reconciliation process included the use of a catch-all to-do list, where we transferred items that didn't have specific deadlines or timeframes for future reference. Items that have specific deadlines or desired timeframes were captured on the calendar. But such items can be alternatively captured in a separate short-term to-do list, which needs then to be reconciled as part of the end-of-day reconciliation process. We also discussed some of the advantages of using the calendar as opposed to a separate to-do list for such items.

The reconciliation process can be one of most productive periods of our day in which we complete items that we intended to do throughout the day but couldn't. In addition, we complete items that came up unexpectedly during the day and that we captured in the journal instead of allowing them to interrupt our flow.

For some people, the end-of-day reconciliation is a 10 to 15 minute process. For others, it may be an hour or more of intense work, especially those who get one or two hundred emails per day, attend back to back meetings and phone conferences, and are dealing with many complex issues and initiatives. Having a structured end-of-day reconciliation process can help make our work efficient and rewarding instead of being overwhelming and frustrating. If you have back to back meetings all day, make it a point to cancel or delegate one of the afternoon meetings, and replace it with the end-of-day reconciliation process.

As we mentioned at the beginning of this chapter, some users are unable to do the end-of-day reconciliation right before they leave at the end of the day because of unexpected last-minute requests that come up. If this is your situation, you may be more successful by scheduling a midafternoon session instead of end-of-day session. The exact time doesn't matter. What matters is taking that time to make the reconciliation process happen.

End-of-day reconciliation, a core activity

The end-of-day reconciliation process, when we approach it with the no-way-out attitude and the intention of getting closure on the issues at hand, prompts the issues and gives us the opportunity to act now instead of postponing and prolonging these tasks. The end of day reconciliation is not an extra chore, but a core activity, in which we get things accomplished and be better positioned to have a positive impact and achieve meaningful results.

Action Plan

Identify the action items that you would like to take as a result of what was covered in this chapter. Indicate the timeframe in which you plan on taking these actions. Then report on the actual date in which you implemented them and a brief note about the results.

Table 1: Action Plan

Practice/Technique	I will start implementing this on (date?)	Actual start date	Actual end date	Comment/Results
Creating the catch-all to-do list and using it				
Reserving 30 to 45 minutes for the end-of-day reconciliation				
Emptying the inbox every single day and handling today's messages				
Reviewing the calendar at the end of each day				
Reviewing journal pages at the end of each day				
Add your own item:				
Add your own item:				
Add your own item:				

Chapter 6: Every Day is A Fresh Day—reconcile at the beginning of each day

How do most of us start our day? When we ask our workshop participants this question, the answer we invariably get is: "on e-mail." Here are some of the reasons why we start the day on e-mail (and why we keep going back to e-mail every time we hear the beep or when we are at a loss of what to do next):

1. Curiosity: We are curious about what happened in the world since we checked e-mail last.

2. Hope for good news: This is the winning-the-lottery syndrome. It may happen to me! I may get this great promotion or great deal or great surprise from someone.

3. Feeling accomplished: Replying to e-mails gives us the feeling that we are getting things done. Each e-mail message answered is like a micro-project successfully completed and checked off the list.

4. Fear of being left behind: We want to make sure we are not missing important information or developments, and potentially losing our competitive edge.

5. Anxiety about outstanding tasks: We cannot relax if we have outstanding e-mail messages.

6. Avoidance: Instead of focusing on more important and usually more difficult tasks, it is easier to be on e-mail.

7. Lack of direction/Need for direction: We don't know exactly what we should be doing, e-mail give us the answer, at least a temporary fix.

8. Handling urgent stuff: We have to check e-mail because we get urgent requests on e-mail, which need to be handled immediately.

9. Meeting the expectations of others: It is usually expected that e-mails are answered fairly quickly, either by our boss, colleagues, or generally as part of the culture in our organization. If we don't meet these expectations, we may be seen as "not fully on top of things."

And there are probably more reasons. All together, these factors make e-mail seductive, addictive, rewarding, and anxiety-provoking, all at the same time.

But e-mail is also our main means of communication. It allows us to do great things. The Accomplishing More With Less Methodology does not blame e-mail for our inefficiencies, but it recognizes that we have developed behaviors around e-mail which, instead of fully leveraging this efficient medium, are turning it into a huge time and energy waste, and significantly increasing its cost-benefit ratio. My goal is to encourage and facilitate behavioral changes that can help you turn this around.

In this chapter, I will introduce the beginning of day reconciliation process, which also consists of three important activities that need to be handled at the beginning of the day.

First Beginning-of-Day Activity: Starting with the journal

Instead of starting the day with e-mail, how about starting it with the journal? Open your journal to a new page, and write down today's date, and then write down a brief outline of what we intend to accomplish today, as shown below:

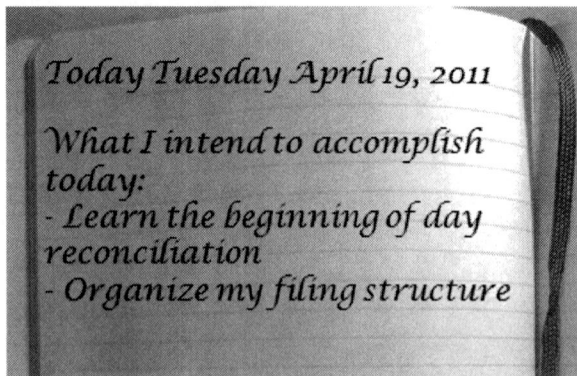

Today Tuesday April 19, 2011

What I intend to accomplish today:
- Learn the beginning of day reconciliation
- Organize my filing structure

Figure 1: Today's Page--what I intend to accomplish today

Then start the Capture Page, and again as we explained in the journal chapter, use this page to jot down to-do items and ideas that you encounter throughout the day, and that you don't want to handle immediately, but rather capture and handle at a time when it is more convenient.

Figure 2: Capture Page

And finally, start the "Notes" page, where you capture meetings notes, phone conversion notes, thinking and strategizing notes.

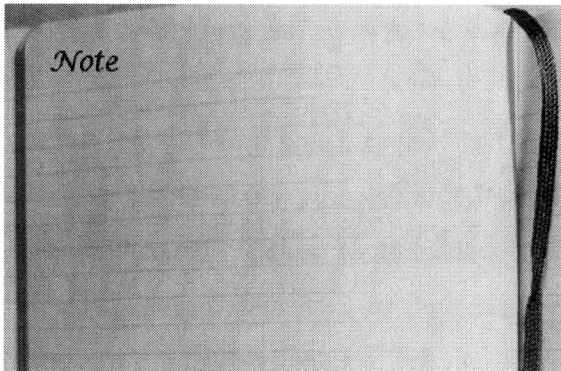

Figure 3: Notes Page

One common question we get in the workshop is: "Why do I need to write down what I intend to accomplish today when I already have these items on my calendar, or my to-do list?"

If you are comfortable with what is on your calendar and/or to-do list, and feel that they adequately represent what you want to accomplish today, then you can skip this step. However, before you decide to skip this step, continue reading and make your decision later.

Here are some of the advantages of stopping, reflecting, and writing down what we intend to accomplish today in the journal:

1. There are strong forces constantly pulling us towards leading a "robotic" work life highly driven by e-mail, instant messaging, meetings, and an array of interruptions, mostly outside our control. Stopping and reflecting on what we want to accomplish each day is our antidote to this interruption driven out-of-control existence. It is the first and necessary step we need to take if we are to exercise some degree of control over our destiny, if we want to be more purposeful, and channel our energy into the right places.

2. We tend to be driven by structured data, and there is plenty of it around to keep us busy, but then we lose touch with our intuitive thinking. Our intuition is likely to have rich information and valuable insights that we are not leveraging. When we stop to reflect on what we want to accomplish today we create just enough space to allow our intuition to surface and help us make better decisions about what we should be focusing our energy on now.

3. We live in a very dynamic world. It has been said, and rightfully so, that the only element that doesn't change is change itself. Our calendar and to-do list are relatively static. As soon as we put items on our calendar or to-do list these items are already outdated at least to some degree, because the world has already changed, at least a bit, and sometimes even drastically. Only by stopping and reflecting, we can realize more fully what has changed, and be in a position to make the necessary adjustments, and take better actions.

Being purposeful, listening to our intuition, and constantly adjusting to an ever changing world, are imperative measures that can help us accomplish more in less time, less effort, and less stress, and lead happier work and personal lives. Starting our day by writing down what we intend to accomplish today is a powerful way to unleash these forces and put them into gear each and every day.

How long does it take?

Reflecting on what we intend to accomplish today and jotting it down can be quick and easy on certain days, while it may be more involved on other days. This depends on the nature of the issues we are dealing with at the moment, the phase we are at in our projects and initiatives, the level and scope of our roles and responsibilities, among other things.

This process however is supposed to be relatively quick. We are talking about minutes here and ideally just a few minutes (just enough to give us a chance to identify what is important for today, and help align our actions with what is truly going on in the world around us). These minutes are a small investment that is likely to bring enormous returns.

Second Beginning-of-Day Activity: Reconciling the calendar

Now that we have purposefully defined what we want to accomplish today, it is time to take a look at our calendar, get mentally prepared for the day, and potentially make adjustments based on what we intend to accomplish today.

As Susan stopped and reflected on what she wanted to accomplish today, she remembered the project meeting she participated in yesterday, and some of the comments that were made by the project team. She realized that there might have been some concerns that weren't fully discussed during the meeting. Susan added one more item on her Today's page relating to this project.

Then when reconciling her calendar, Susan scheduled a conference call with the key project team members to address these concerns. In order to make room for this conference call, she had to postpone another meeting. This helped Susan and the project team proactively address important project and personnel issues which would have otherwise become difficult to manage later in the project.

Third Beginning-of-Day Activity: Handling labeled messages

The third part of the beginning-of-day reconciliation relates to e-mail. Knowing that we already handled the messages labeled for today when we did yesterday's end-of-day reconciliation, our goal now is to handle the messages labeled for tomorrow and those that we are waiting for others to handle. As you recall from our e-mail chapter, these messages were labels as "2 Tomorrow" and "3 Waiting For." Now is the time to visit these labels:

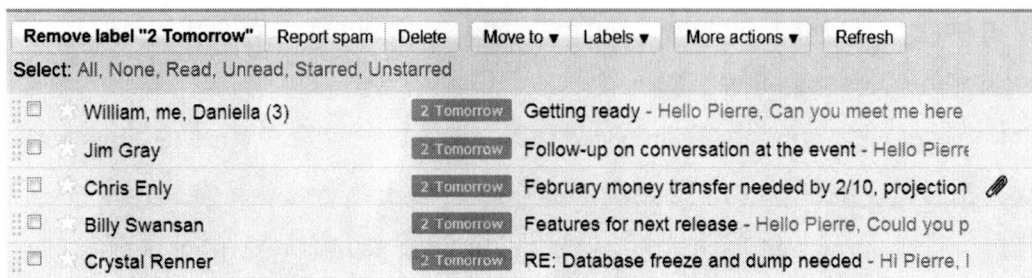

Figure 4: Blue and Yellow Flags

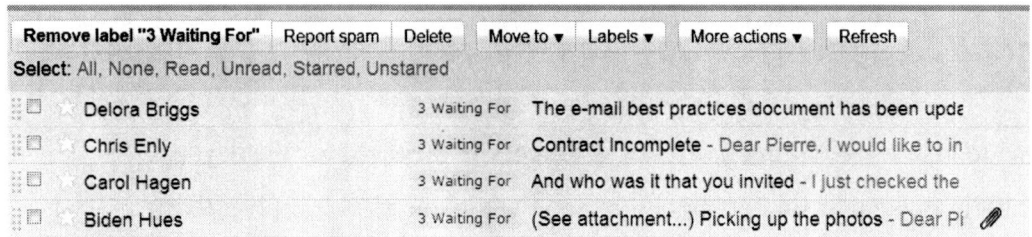

Figure 5: Blue and Yellow Flags

As I go through these messages, I immediately handle the ones that I can easily handle, move to "1 Today" the ones that are becoming more urgent and that I would like to handle later today, and leave the remaining message where they are. The question is: "Do I need to come back to these messages again today?" The answer is a definite no. By definition these messages are messages that don't need to be handled today. That is why we assigned them the "2 Tomorrow" or "3 Waiting For" labels in the first place.

Using the "2 Tomorrow" and "3 Waiting For" labels is an important boost to our productivity. If we don't assign these labels to these messages, such messages would otherwise be scattered throughout our inbox; they would clutter our inbox and hide important messages. In addition, they would distract us and hamper our ability to stay focused.

And now into the inbox

Now is the time to get into the inbox and go through new messages. We will handle the urgent ones and the ones that can be easily and quickly handled, while assigning the appropriate labels and archiving other messages.

Some workshop participants tell us that they must start their day by reviewing the inbox, as opposed to the beginning-of-day reconciliation process we described above, because they get urgent messages overnight or early in the morning which may need immediate attention or may change how they plan the day. This usually applies to customer service, support, and sales related functions. If this is the case, you may tailor your beginning-of-day reconciliation process to include checking urgent messages first (whether e-mail or voice mail or whatever way they get to you), and then going through the steps outlined above. Be careful though! Once you start with the inbox, there is an overwhelming temptation to open messages of all kinds, and find yourself two hours later still in the inbox.

Beginning-of-day reconciliation in review

The beginning-of-day reconciliation process may take 5 or 10 minutes on certain days and longer on other days. This time however is not time spent but time invested with same-day returns. Writing down what we intend to accomplish today helps us, consciously and subconsciously, stay on track throughout the day. It helps us put the stake in the ground and hold ourselves accountable. It also gives us the opportunity to rethink our day and take action to influence what is happening instead of being blindly driven by what is on our calendar and what is in e-mail. Finally, our e-mail labels save us significant time and energy by helping us group messages together in holding areas instead of having them in our way at all times. Most importantly, the beginning of day reconciliation help us create the state of mind that we need in order to lead a more productive and happy day.

Action Plan

Identify the action items that you would like to take as a result of what was covered in this chapter. Indicate the timeframe in which you plan on taking these actions. Then report on the actual date in which you implemented them and a brief note about the results.

Table 1: Action Plan

Practice/Technique	I will start implementing this on (date?)	Actual start date	Actual end date	Comment/Results
Start a new page in the journal and write what I intend to accomplish today				
Review my calendar at the beginning of the day and make adjustments if necessary				
Review the "2 Tomorrow" and "3 Waiting For" messages and handle or escalate those that require attention				
Add your own item:				
Add your own item:				
Add your own item:				

Chapter 7: Finding information easily when you need it!

Most business professionals are overwhelmed by the amount of information they have to handle. They spend a significant amount of time trying to manage it and search for it when they need it.

When we have a well-designed filing structure, we are likely to be able to file (or label) information easier and find it faster. But there is more to it. A well designed filing structure helps us think more clearly about our priorities and stay focused on what is important, as we will see shortly.

From Folders to Labels

Why even mention filing in Gmail and Google Apps? Didn't they do away with filing all together? At the surface, it may seem that filing is not relevant anymore, but as you dig deeper, you realize that it is just as relevant and useful as it has ever been. Gmail didn't do away with filing per se, but enhanced it using labels. Labels are more flexible than traditional folders. They solved one of the long standing dilemmas that users have been complaining about for years: "How do I file information that seems to belong in two or more folders?" Gmail allows you to apply labels to your heart's content; you can apply multiple labels to the same information. In addition, one of the Gmail labs enables you to have nested labels allowing labels to have a hierarchy similar to what traditional folders offer.

Therefore, the issue of "why even address the topic of filing in Gmail and Google Apps" is a mute issue. Furthermore, most users still manage a host of other documents that reside on hard drives, shared drives, and in paper folders--and therefore have to deal with some form of filing or another. Most importantly, as we briefly mentioned above, a well-designed filing structure helps us think more clearly about our priorities and stay focused on what is important! So let us proceed with creating a filing structure that is optimized for our needs and then apply it selectively to our e-mail labels, hard drive folders, and paper folders.

Sample Structure

When it came to labeling e-mail, Christine did not do much. She left her e-mails in her inbox and didn't bother to archive them nor label them. Her Gmail labels were as follows:

E-mail Labels

Figure 1: E-mail filing structure

Her hard drive structure on the other hand took a life of its own. Christine kept adding folders in an ad-hoc fashion:

Hard Drive Folders

Finance
　Business
　　Analysis
　　Process
　　Projections
　　Tax Forms
　　Templates
　Nancy
　Personal
Hiring
　CEO
　Forms
　India
　Marketing
　　Marketing Director
　　Marketing Managers
　　VP of Marketing
　Professional Services
　　Consultants
　　Managers
　Recruiters
　SalesReps
　　Paula
　　Kenny
　　Brenda
Mail
Marketing
　Conferences
　　DCI Bostong
　　DCI SF
　　DMA LA
　Customer ROI
　Digital Postcards
　Direct Marketing
　Market Research
　Marketing Features

Marketing Plan
　Direct Marketing
　Product Marketing
　Public Relations
Marketing Programs
Partnerships
Presentations
　Company 1
　Company 2
　Etc.
Public Relations
　Agencies
　Analysis
　Presentations
Seminars
　Content
　Content Updates
　Logistics
　Evaluations
Products
　Advisory Board
　Beta Specs
　Competitive Analysis
　Customers
　Demo Scripts
　Design
　Features
　Overseas Development
Sales
　Sales Goals
　Sales Planning
　Sales Proposals
　Sales Reps
　Sales Toolkit
Strategic
　Acquisitions
　Andrew
　Company Board Meetings
　　Meeting 11-01

Mgmt Meetings
　Offsite 03-01
　Weekly mtgs
　Etc.
Team Meetings
　Events
　Funding
　Market Analysis
　Org. Development
　Positioning
　Priorities
　Thinking
Tactical
　Brown Bag Lunches
　Friday Morning Mtgs
　Legal
　License Agreements
　Office Move
　Payroll
　Performance Reviews
　Roles and Goals
　　Employee 1
　　Employee 2
　　Etc.
　Quarter 1-01
　Quarter 2-01
　Etc.
Vacations
Training
　Workshops
　Executive Education
　Brown Bags
　　Effective Meetings
　　Software Life Cycle
　Toastmasters
　Trips

Figure 2: Hard drive filing structure

Christine did not deal with a lot of paper. Her paper folders were as follows:

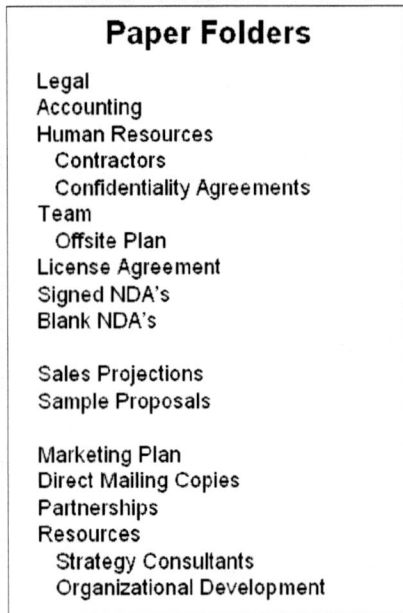

Paper Folders

Legal
Accounting
Human Resources
  Contractors
  Confidentiality Agreements
Team
  Offsite Plan
License Agreement
Signed NDA's
Blank NDA's

Sales Projections
Sample Proposals

Marketing Plan
Direct Mailing Copies
Partnerships
Resources
  Strategy Consultants
  Organizational Development

Figure 3: Paper filing structure

The New and Improved Information Architecture

To help Christine improve her filing structure, we applied three filing

concepts, and the following new structure emerged:

E-mail Labels

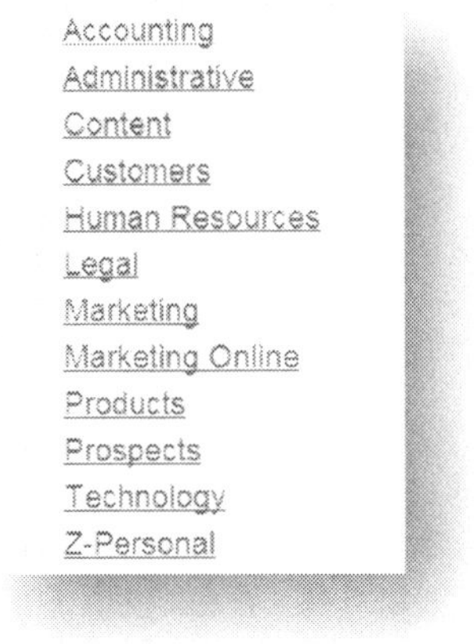

Accounting
Administrative
Content
Customers
Human Resources
Legal
Marketing
Marketing Online
Products
Prospects
Technology
Z-Personal

Figure 4: Improved e-mail labels

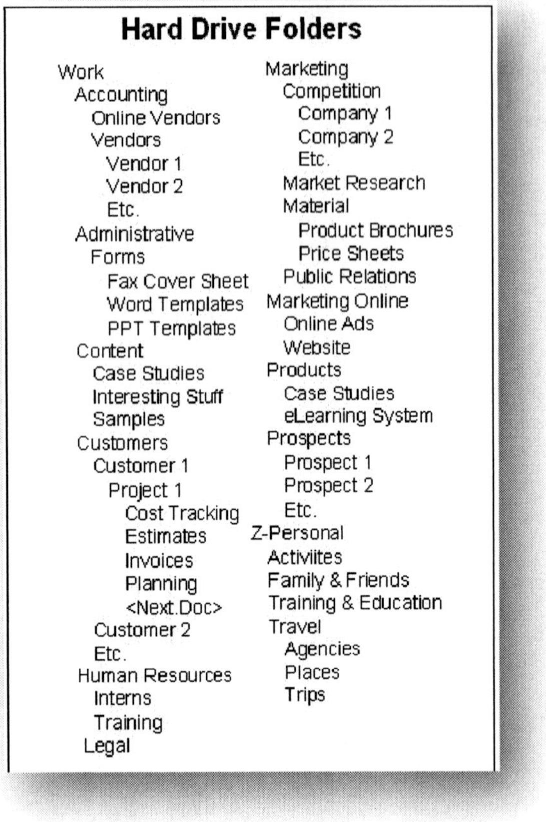

Hard Drive Folders

Work
  Accounting
    Online Vendors
  Vendors
    Vendor 1
    Vendor 2
    Etc.
  Administrative
    Forms
      Fax Cover Sheet
      Word Templates
      PPT Templates
  Content
    Case Studies
    Interesting Stuff
    Samples
  Customers
    Customer 1
      Project 1
        Cost Tracking
        Estimates
        Invoices
        Planning
        <Next.Doc>
    Customer 2
    Etc.
  Human Resources
    Interns
    Training
  Legal

Marketing
  Competition
    Company 1
    Company 2
    Etc.
  Market Research
  Material
    Product Brochures
    Price Sheets
  Public Relations
Marketing Online
  Online Ads
  Website
Products
  Case Studies
  eLearning System
Prospects
  Prospect 1
  Prospect 2
  Etc.
Z-Personal
  Activiites
  Family & Friends
  Training & Education
  Travel
    Agencies
    Places
    Trips

Figure 5: Improved hard drive filing structure

Paper Folders

Work
  Accounting
    Business Exp Rec.
    Project Exp Rec.
  Administrative
  Content
  Customers
    Customer 1
      Project 1
      Project 2
    Customer 2
    Etc.
  Human Resources
    Colleagues
      Barb
      Howard
      Etc.
    Training
      Leadership
      Communications
      Technical
  Legal
    Incorporation
    Stockholders
    License Agreem.
  Marketing
    Articles
    Associations
      AMA
      ASTD

  Conferences
    TechLaunch 03
    Etc.
  Marketing Material
    Postcard Info
  Seminars
    Hotels/Rooms
    Etc.
Products
  Product 1
    Offsite
  Prospects
    Prospect 1
    Etc.
  Technology
    Computers
      Asset 1
      Etc.
    Electronics
      Asset 1
      Etc.r
Z-Personal
  Activiltes
  Family & Friends
  Training & Education
  Travel
    Agencies
    Places
    Trips

Figure 6: Improved paper filing structure

Turn to a new page in the journal, write down today's date, and what you want to accomplish today which is "Organize my filing structure." Start the Capture Page to capture the myriad of items that come up during the day so they don't interrupt your flow. Then start the Notes pages to capture meeting notes.

If you review the enhanced structures shown above, and compare them with the original structures Christine had originally as shown earlier in this chapter, what do you notice? Take a few minutes to jot down your observations in your journal before you read on.

Concept one: One structure

Take a look at the improved e-mail labels above. You notice that we have Accounting, Administrative, Content, Customers, Human Resources, Legal, Marketing, etc.

Now review the work folder in the improved hard drive structure, and you notice that we have the same folders: Accounting, Administrative, Content, Customers, Human Resources, Legal, Marketing, etc. and if you take a look at the improved paper folders, you will find the same folders.

In other words, we have "one" filing structure that is consistently applied to the three mediums (e-mail, hard drive, and paper). After all, we have the same goals and responsibilities and deal with similar information irrelevant of which medium we are working in.

When designing our "one" filing structure, there are several important top level folders to consider:

1. Customers

2. Products and services

3. Internal team

4. External audiences (partners, vendors, and suppliers)

5. Content (or knowledge-base)

6. Administrative

Most filing structures are likely to include the above folders or some variation thereof. Your customers may be internal customers if you are part of the internal helpdesk team of an organization, or they may be faculty or students if you are in an educational institution. Your content folders may be your research topics if you are part of a research team. You need to adapt these folders and label them appropriately based on your environment and preferences.

Shortly I will suggest a couple of approaches to help you define your own filing structure. For now, I would like to continue with the design concepts.

Concept two: Apply the structure on an as-needed basis

If you take a look at Christine's improved hard drive filing structure (Figure 5), and review the Customers folder and subfolders, and then compare them to the Customers folder and subfolders in the paper folders (Figure 6), what do you notice?

In the improved hard drive filing structure, the Customers subfolders are broken down by customer, and then by project, and within each project, there are subfolders for each area of the project, such as Cost Tracking, Estimates, Invoices, Planning, etc. In the improved paper folders however, the structure is not broken down to this granular level.

This is where concept two comes into play: Apply the filing structure on an as-needed basis. This means that if we don't need certain folders in a certain medium, we don't create blank folders just for the sake of consistency. But if and when the need arises, we can easily add these folders. For instance, Christine does not currently need the Cost Tracking paper folder, but if she starts to receive some paper documents relating to cost tracking, she can easily add the Cost Tacking folder to her paper folders and stay consistent with her other mediums.

Concept three: Let each medium do what it does best

We are dealing with three different mediums here: E-mail, hard drive, and paper. The third concept states "let each medium do what it does best." Instead of having the same information handled and stored in multiple mediums, concept three calls for optimizing our usage of each medium and minimizing duplication.

What is e-mail best at? When we ask this question at our workshops, participants quickly provide the correct answer: Communication. What does our hard drive do best? The answer doesn't seem as easy in this case. Storage is what comes to almost everyone's mind. Hard drives are great at storage, but there is one thing that they are "best" at. And that is for "authoring" and "editing." It is where we create documents and where we edit documents. Finally, what is paper best at? Storage, archive, and backup are common answers, but the more accurate response is storing "originals." Our paper files are primarily for storing information that cannot be otherwise reproduced. This may include documents that have signatures, handwritten notes, or documents that came to us as paper that we cannot otherwise reproduce.

If we use each of these mediums based on what they do best, instead of using them in an ad-hoc fashion and storing the same information in multiple places, two important things will happen. First, we will have a lot less information to organize, file, and store. Second, we will have less information to search when we need it later.

Let us apply this last concept to some real-life situations. Susan likes to print certain e-mails and certain documents so that she can read them on paper instead of electronically. This give her the opportunity to get away from the computer screen, maybe even sit on a comfortable chair away from the computer, and read more carefully, flipping through the pages back and forth as she refers to different sections.

When Susan is done with the printout, what should she do with it? According to the above concept, the e-mail or the document belongs to the electronic medium, and the printout is nothing but a duplicate which can be reproduced at any time. Therefore ideally, Susan will throw the printout in the recycling or shredding bin.

What if Susan jots down some notes on the printout as she reads the document? The document now becomes an original and can now be filed in the paper folders if these notes are important for future reference. However, if Susan transfers the handwritten notes someplace else, then the printout is a duplicate again, and should be recycled or shredded.

The above example demonstrates the types of questions we want to ask ourselves as we handle information so we can more efficiently manage these mediums.

Exercise 1: Designing your structure, the top down approach

Now it is time to get to work. The goal of this exercise and the following exercise is to come up with a filing structure that best fits our needs and makes it easier to label, file, and find information in any medium.

Use the Notes section of your notebook for this exercise. First you will come up with the top level folders of your new structure. The idea here is to take a step back, put your existing filing structure on the side for the time being, and come up with an the ideal filing structure that would best fit your needs.

So which filing structure are we talking about? Is it e-mail labels, hard drive folders, or paper folders? That was a trick question! Remember, it is "one" filing structure. So we need to let go of thinking about the mediums for the time being and think about "information architecture."

If you take a look at the enhanced structure above, you see that the labels and top level folder are: Accounting, Administrative, Content, Customers, Human Resources, Legal, Marketing, etc. So the question in this exercise is: "What would these be for you?"

Once you come up with what you think the top level is in your ideal filing structure would be, let us address a few common issues that usually come up in the workshop.

A common question is: "How many items should we have at the top level?" 3 items at the top level are probably too few and 15 are probably too many. We recommend that you keep it to 10 or less. The top level is supposed to represent the important areas of our information architecture, and not be an exhaustive list of all the information we deal with.

Patrick, a project manager at a technology company, had more than 20 top level items. When we reviewed them together, we concluded that the key projects, which he put at the top level, can be grouped together under one top level item called projects. If you're finding yourself with many top level items, it is likely that some of them can be grouped together.

Your next level of items

Once you are done with the top level, the next step would be to come up with the next level items. At this point, we are thinking information architecture. So even if you are not planning on labeling e-mail messages or using nested labels, it is still important to continue with this exercise and break down the structure further so that your information architecture continues to get refined.

Take a few minutes to jot down the sub-items that come to your mind within each top level item. We will get a chance to refine and complete the list later when we get to exercise 2. If and as necessary, you might even take this exercise a step further, and continue with expanding the structure to the third level.

A question that comes up often is: "How many levels deep should the filing structure go?" Overall, we are aiming at being minimalistic and at continuing to think 80/20. This means the fewer levels the better. However when it comes to the core areas of our business (the 20%) we want to have the levels that are necessary to label or file the information appropriately and find it efficiently. We don't want to sacrifice clarity and efficiency to cut down on levels.

Exercise 2: Designing your structure, the bottom-up approach

This exercise will help us finish the structure that we started in the first exercise. In this exercise, you need to print out your existing structure (the hard drive filing structure is likely to be the most effective here) and use the printout as indicated below.

Using the printout, review your existing filing structure, and for each folder, determine if the folder is still in use. If not, cross it off. If it is in use, then a) decide if it needs to be renamed, and b) if it needs to be moved to a more appropriate location in the structure. This is an opportunity to rename folders clearly and consistently and most importantly to continue to evolve and refine the structure that we started in the first exercise, as illustrated in the example below.

Here is a quick example from Delora who had the following folders in her filing structure (we are only showing the Strategic folder and its subfolders just to illustrate a few points):

Existing Folders/Subfolders

- Strategic
  - Acquisitions
  - Andrew
  - Company Board Meetings
  - Team Meetings
  - Events
  - Funding
  - Market Analysis
  - Org. Development
  - Positioning
  - Priorities
  - Thinking

Figure 7: Existing Strategic folder and its subfolders (part of the printout)

Delora went through these folders and this is how she marked her printout:

Adjustments to Folders/Subfolders

	New Names	New Locations
• Strategic		
— Acquisitions		
— Andrew	Andrew Bielefeld	Staff > Consultants
— Co. Board Meetings	Board Meetings	
— Team Meetings		
— Events		Functional > Marketing
— Funding		Financial
— Market Analysis	Market Research	Functional > Marketing
— Org. Development	Development	Staff
— Positioning		
— Priorities		
— Thinking	Planning	

Figure 8: Adjustments made on the printout

As you can see, Delora for instance, decided to rename the folder "Andrew" to "Andrew Bielefeld"--starting a new naming convention of using both first and last names when handling information relating to people. Then she realized that the work that she does with Andrew Bielefeld does not relate to strategic initiatives and issues and therefore should be moved to a different folder. Andrew Bielefeld is a consultant working on HR related projects so she decided to have a folder for consultants (to be named Consultants) and make it a subfolder within a top level folder for staff (to be named Staff).

At this point, Delora took a look at the structure that she designed in the first exercise above, and made sure that the folder Staff was included as a top level folder, and that Consultants was a subfolder within it. As you can see, this exercise allowed Delora not only to clean up her old and unused folders and rename her current folder more clearly and consistently, but also to complete the design of her new and improved filing structure which we started in the previous exercise. When she completes this exercise she will have in her possession the blueprint for the new and improved filing structure.

How long does this take?

Even if you have hundreds of folders, the above exercise is not likely to take more than an hour or so. Once you get started and go through the first set of folders, it is likely that you will pick up momentum, make faster decisions and go through the folders quickly and easily. Something to keep in mind is that our goal is to simplify the structure and apply the 80/20 rule, so that the resulting structure is refined and optimized. For most business professionals, this is an opportunity to get rid of old information and unnecessary details.

Implementing the new structure

The outcome of the above two exercises is a filing structure that is up-to-date and optimized to best serve your needs. Now it is time to implement the new structure in our three mediums, based on the three concepts we discussed earlier: 1) One filing structure 2) Apply the structure on an as-needed basis, and 3) Let each medium do what it does best.

The New e-mail labels

This consists of creating labels for the top level items in the improved structure. You may even decide to use the nested labels and create labels for the second level items and beyond. The goal is not to label all e-mail messages but only the top 20% that relate to the important results that we are trying to accomplish. The rest of the messages can be archived and later retrieved via search or found in the All Mail label if needed.

New hard drive filing structure

This consists of creating a new top level folder on your hard drive and calling it "Work", or "New Structure", or "New Beginning", or whatever name you find appropriate. Then you create the new filing structure within this new top level folder. Now that you have this new structure, every time you open an existing document from your old structure, you save it in the new structure. Therefore, the documents that are still in use will gradually migrate to the new structure. Obviously when you create new documents, you create them in the new structure. You can keep your old structure for some time and later archive it to another storage device.

New paper filing structure

Implementing the new structure in the paper folders can be more involved than the electronic world because we need to put the existing paper folders on the side to create room for the new folders. However the process is basically the same. Some users who deal with important papers find it worthwhile to go through the existing paper folders and bring the important and current documents to the new paper folders at once. Other users put most of the existing paper folders in storage boxes and then selectively move folders when necessary.

Frequently raised issues

Work versus personal

This question is bound to come up in every workshop and in every conversation relating to filing information: Is it best to separate work information from personal information, or keep them together? This includes items in e-mail, calendar, to-do lists, hard drive, paper folder, and the like.

We are finding that the lines between work and personal are becoming less and less defined. In today's information age, knowledge workers are finding themselves conducting business after hours, accessing their information online 24x7, and working virtually with people around the globe. Similarly, they are taking care of personal items during business hours using their work computers, and many are finding it more convenient to keep work and personal information together.

One thing to be reminded of however is that most companies have e-policies which indicate that any information kept on company systems is subject to review by the company or is even the property of the company. E-policies also tend to restrict the amount of time that employees can spend on personal items, some being very strict, while others indicating that this time should be kept to a minimum and not interfere with the employee's ability to conduct their business activities. While companies aren't likely to review employees' personal information, if problems arise, they are likely to audit this information and use it. Employees are encouraged to use good judgment and be aware of their company's e-policy when it comes to personal use and storage of personal information.

Search versus Label

This is yet another common question that relates to the issue of whether it is important to label e-mail messages, knowing that search can easily find them when we need it. While we already addressed this issue in the e-mail chapter earlier, here are a few relevant insights.

With the e-mail volume becoming increasingly overwhelming, more users are opting not to label e-mail messages and just archive them. We find that this approach, of search-instead-of-label, works well when you try to find messages that fit your search criteria well. The more specifics you know about the message, the more likely search will find it quickly and easily. This approach isn't as efficient however when you only have a vague idea of what you are looking for. In this case, you may go through several searches and have to browse through several search results before you find what you want, and sometimes you may not even find it.

The approach that we recommend is a hybrid approach that leverages the best of both worlds (the "search" world and the "labeling" world). This consist of labeling only core message – the top 20%, and using search to find information in the remaining 80% – which meanwhile can be simply archived.

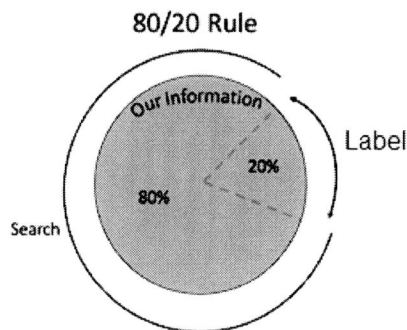

Figure 9: Label 20% and use search to find 80%

The group filing structure

Many teams tend to have shared network drives and keep shared documents on these drives in order to facilitate access to these documents and better manage the process of updating these documents. The question that comes up relates to what filing structure should be used on these shared drives, and how this structure relates to individual filing structures.

We generally recommend that the team gets together and follows the exercises described in this chapter to design a shared filing structure. This process can start with a brainstorming session about what the ideal filing structure would look like followed by a discussion and agreement on an initial structure (this would be similar to the first exercise in this chapter). Then the team can proceed to print the current structure of the shared drive, review it together, cross off old folders, rename folders more consistently, and decide on where folders should go in the new structure (this would be similar to the second exercise in this chapter).

As a result, the team will have a new shared drive filing structure. Then the individual team members structure can be a "super-set" of the shared filing structure in which team members add the folders that that they need for their own information that is not related to the team work.

Exercise 1: Top level folders and next level folders

For each top level item, include the necessary 2nd level items, and then 3rd level items. Make copies of this form as necessary.

Table 5: Your ideal filing structure

Top Level	2nd Level (3 to 5 items within each top level)	3rd Level (5 to 7 items within each 2nd level)
Name:	Name:	
	Name:	
	Name:	
	Name:	
	Name:	

Action Plan

Identify the action items that you would like to take as a result of what was covered in this chapter. Indicate the timeframe in which you plan on taking these actions. Then report on the actual date in which you implemented them and a brief note about the results.

Table 2: Action Plan

Practice/Technique	I will start implementing this on (date?)	Actual start date	Actual end date	Comment/Results
Designing my new information architecture				
Working with my team to come up with a structure for the shared drive				
Implementing my new structure in e-mail labels				
Implementing my new structure on my hard drive or network drive				
Implementing my new structure for my paper files				
Add your own item:				
Add your own item:				
Add your own item:				

Chapter 8: The Last Priority System You Will Ever Use—manage conflicting priorities with the "matrix"

Turn to a new page in the journal and write down today's date, and what you want to accomplish today which is "managing priorities." Start the Capture Page to capture the myriad of items that come up during the day so they don't interrupt your flow. Then start the Notes pages to capture meeting notes. We are now ready to tackle the topic of conflicting priorities and how we can best manage them.

Listing Your Immediate Priorities

On the Notes Page, list your immediate priorities – items you need to accomplish within the next two weeks. For now, this is a brain dump exercise without much thinking involved. Don't worry about ordering these items or analyzing them. Instead, any item that comes to your mind (large or small, significant project or a small to-do item, personal or work) jot it down on the journal.

The Immediate Priorities Matrix™

I am going to introduce a tool that we call the Immediate Priorities Matrix™. This is a tool you use primarily when you have too many priorities, feel overwhelmed, are not sure where to start, and concerned that you won't be able to get tasks done. They all appear to be urgent and equally important and you find yourself unable to focus on any one task and make much progress. This is exactly where the Immediate Priorities Matrix ™ comes to the rescue.

Even though our primary purpose of introducing this tool is to help you manage these challenging times, this tool is equally helpful when it comes to pre-planning. We will touch more on this topic in the following chapter.

In the exercise above, Mark jotted down the following items as his immediate priorities:

Note

My priorities
- Ally Technologies
- Applied Engineering
- At-Tech Conference marketing material
- Budget update
- Partnership agreement with Timothy

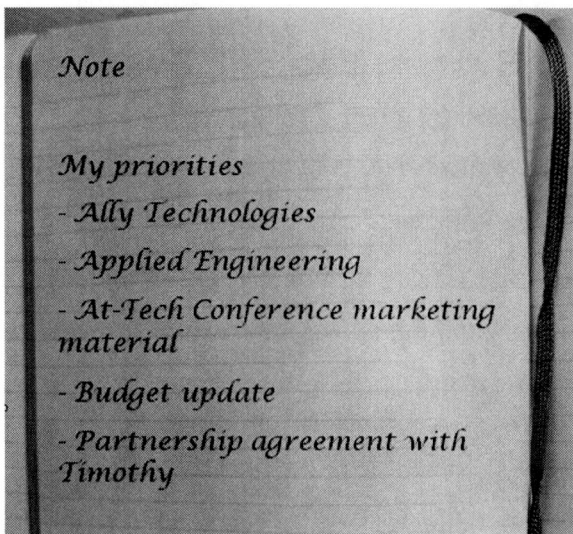

We will use the Immediate Priorities Matrix™ to help Mark better manage his priorities. The Immediate Priorities Matrix™ involves the following information organized in a table (matrix-like) format:

Table 1: Immediate Priorities Matrix™ format

Priority	Breakdown	Immediate/ Next Actions	Estimated Time	Deadline

In the first row and first column, let us put the first priority, which is one of Mark's customers (Ally Technologies):

Table 2: First priority

Priority	Breakdown	Immediate/ Next Actions	Estimated Time	Deadline
Ally Technologies				

In the second column, let us break it down into the steps that are involved in completing this priority:

Table 3: First priority breakdown

Priority	Breakdown	Immediate/ Next Actions	Estimated Time	Deadline
Ally technologies	Install new software Plan first session Update Joan & team Send material to printer Train the trainer Schedule final dates			

In the third column, let us identify the steps that are truly immediate and that need to be handled first so other steps can follow:

Table 4: Identifying the immediate

Priority	Breakdown	Immediate/ Next Actions	Estimated Time	Deadline
Ally technologies	Install new software Plan first session Update Joan & team Send material to printer Train the trainer Schedule final dates	Install new software Ask Joan for dates		

In the next column, we need to estimate how long it would take to perform the immediate steps. The final column is where we indicate the deadline or target completion date for the immediate steps.

Table 5: Estimating duration and identifying timeframe

Priority	Breakdown	Immediate/ Next Actions	Estimated Time	Deadline
Ally technologies	Install new software Plan first session Update Joan & team Send material to printer Train the trainer Schedule final dates	Install new software Ask Joan for dates	60 min 5 min	Monday Mar 21

Mark completes the matrix by filling in one row for each of his immediate priorities. As a result his Immediate Priorities Matrix™ is as follows:

Table 6: Completed Immediate Priorities Matrix™

Priority	Breakdown	Immediate/ Next Actions	Estimated Time	Deadline
Ally technologies	Install new software Plan first session Update Joan & team Send material to printer Train the trainer Schedule final dates	Install new software Ask Joan for dates	60 min 5 min	Monday Mar 21
Applied Engineering	Prepare the content Debrief Christy Update proposal Schedule call with Training director	Prepare the content first pass E-mail Christy	60 min 20 min	Wed Mar 23
Ad-Tech Conference marketing material	Finish the program outline and description Send it to conference coordinator for review Ask Christine to proof it Send to printer	Finish outline and description Send it to conference coordinator	60 min 10 min	Wed Mar 23
Budget update	Review latest input Update sales projections Finalize new hosted services agreements Send to Joan for her input	Plan what is needed, who will be contributing to this process, and delegate accordingly	2 hours	Thu Mar 24
Partnership agreement with Timothy	Review agreement with legal Update marketing material based on latest discussion Send to Christine to proof and layout Finalize and sign agreement	Update Timothy, and ask for an additional week	5 min	Thu Mar 24

A sigh of relief

At this point in time, and once the Immediate Priorities Matrix™ is filled out, participants experience a sigh of relief. When we put the above items on paper, as opposed to leaving them floating or racing in a disorderly fashion in our mind, we feel better and we are in a much better position to deal with them. In addition, breaking things down into smaller components can help us plan and execute more efficiently.

Furthermore, the Immediate Priorities Matrix™ goes a step further, and includes a deadline or target date for the immediate or next action items, which enables us to move forward to systematically schedule these immediate action items as we will demonstrate shortly. This frees us from the paralysis or frenzy that we may experience when we are faced with these priorities all at once.

Stopping and preparing the Immediate Priorities Matrix™ is a powerful response to the madness that may be going on around us. It gives us the desperately needed opportunity to notice what is really going on and reflect on it. It also lays the foundation needed to determine what to do now and what to do next. This is a very empowering exercise which gives us a sense of being in control instead of feeling driven uncontrollably by the waterfall of external circumstances.

From matrix to calendar

Our work with the Immediate Priorities Matrix™ is far from over. Actually, it has just begun. What we have done so far is the prep work and now it is time to put the Immediate Priorities Matrix™ into use. The next step is to schedule the items from the "Immediate/Next Actions" column on the calendar. This is where the rubber hits the road.

Scheduling these items on the calendar ensures that time is set aside so you don't get caught up with meetings and other activities, but rather have a scheduled time slot applied towards your priorities.

Obviously scheduling is a mechanical process. You sort your list by due date, so that items that are due sooner appear on top. Then you start scheduling the activities on your calendar. Let us demonstrate this process before we dive into some important observations. Let us start with the first row on Mark's Immediate Priorities Matrix™:

Table 7: First priority in the matrix

Priority	Breakdown	Immediate/ Next Actions	Estimated Time	Deadline
Ally technologies	Install new software Plan first session Update Joan & team Send material to printer Train the trainer Schedule final dates	Install new software Ask Joan for dates	60 min 5 min	Monday March 21

Mark needs to get the new software installed by Monday, and this requires an hour of his time, so he reserves an hour for this task on his calendar the Thursday before:

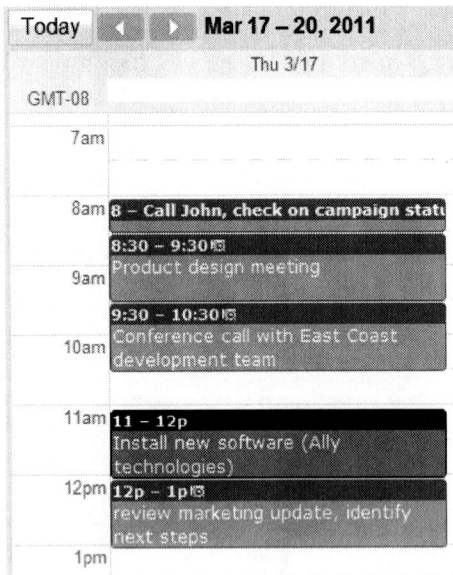

Figure 1: Activity scheduled on the calendar

Then he decides to ask Joan for dates on Friday morning, together with a number of other follow-ups that he plans to do that morning:

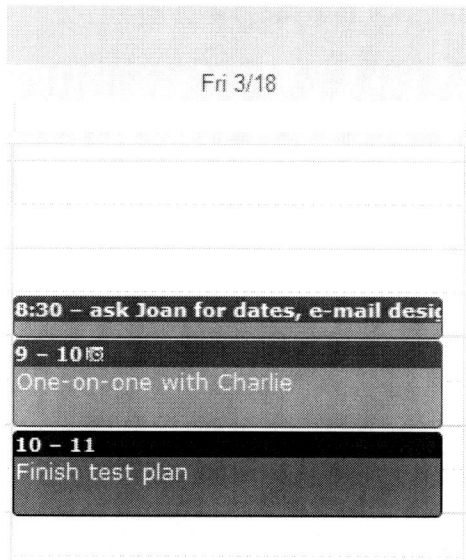

Figure 2: Follow-up scheduled on the calendar

Mark proceeds to schedule the rest of the activities on his Immediate Priorities Matrix™, one activity after another, as described above. In an ideal world he will be able to schedule all the necessary activities within the specified deadlines. However in real life, Mark (and most of us in today's information overload) is likely to "run out of time" and not be able to schedule all the necessary activities. In other words, our calendar is likely to fill up before we are half-way through the matrix. This happened to Mark when he was trying to schedule the budget update:

Table 8: Priority that cannot be scheduled

Budget update	Review latest input Update the sales projections Finalize the new hosted services agreements Send them to Joan for her input	Plan what is needed, and who will be contributing to this process, and delegate accordingly	2 hours	Thu Mar 24

So what should Mark do now? And what should he do with the remaining activities? The answer comes from two important strategies. First is managing expectations. Second is negotiation.

Managing Expectations

Managing expectations starts with informing those who might be impacted by these activities, that they are not going to be completed within the expected timeframes. In the case of the budget update, Mark identifys who is expecting these updates, and who else might be impacted by these updates, and communicates the delay promptly and clearly. Sometimes, this communication is enough and it helps everyone plan their work accordingly. However, sometimes the impact is more significant, and this is where negotiation kicks in.

Negotiation

If delaying the budget update is not acceptable, then Mark needs to put his negotiation hat on, and start to explore ways in which he can help solve this resource conflict. This is where the Immediate Priorities Matrix™ becomes an effective negotiation tool. With the matrix in hand, Mark can point out what other activities are taking up his time and energy, and see if together with the other stakeholders, they can identify areas where he can delay, delegate or adjust scope, in order to make room for the budget update. The Immediate Priorities Matrix™ can turn such negotiation into constructive problem solving sessions where everyone's creativity rises to the occasion and everyone works collaboratively to find a plausible solution. Without the data and objective nature of the Immediate Priorities Matrix™, such discussions can easily get sidetracked and become confrontational and futile.

Keep thinking 80/20

An important concept to keep in mind as we manage expectations and negotiate is the 80/20 rule. Remember that 80% of our results come from 20% of our effort. This can help shed some light on what is truly important, and help make meaningful tradeoffs. One of the activities you have already scheduled on your calendar, can be delayed or cancelled, to make room for another more important activity that is going to yield a much higher return.

But I don't have time

Once in a while, a workshop participant indicates that she already has this information (the information that is supposed to be in the Immediate Priorities Matrix™) in other project documents and therefore questions why she should spend the time to put it in the Immediate Priorities Matrix™, not to mention, there isn't enough time to do so.

The Immediate Priorities Matrix™ is not supposed to replace project management documents or other supporting documents. It is meant to pull the essence of what is going on into one view. It is meant to be succinct (15 or 20 minutes worth of work) and unlike project documents that represent whole projects and whole teams over a period of time, the matrix is a snapshot of what is going on now and up to two weeks from now. Most importantly, it is primarily a rescue tool for those times when you feel overwhelmed. If you are managing well and don't need rescuing from information overload and conflicting demands, then you can just keep it in mind for when you need it; unless (like some workshop participants opt to do) you decide to use it as a planning tool.

Immediate Priorities Matrix™ as a Planning Tool

Why wait to get overwhelmed and in need of rescuing? Why not prepare the matrix regularly or on an as-needed basis, to help us get *one clear view* of what is going on in our world (not our team, not our company, just us), and what is going on now (not now through the life of the project or budget cycle or whatever else, but only now and up to two weeks from now) and plan these important activities on our calendar. Why not be in charge instead of feeling pulled in all directions? This is what many participants discover as they develop the habit of resorting periodically to the Immediate Priorities Matrix™.

Immediate Priorities Matrix Using Google Docs

While some users prefer to use the journal for the matrix, others find it convenient to have it in electronic form. Google Docs can be the ideal place to create the matrix, so when you are setting expectations or negotiating remotely, you will be able to access it easily from anywhere including your mobile device on the go. Here is a sample of the matrix in a document in Google Docs, and later in the book, we will be expanding on the Google Docs capabilities:

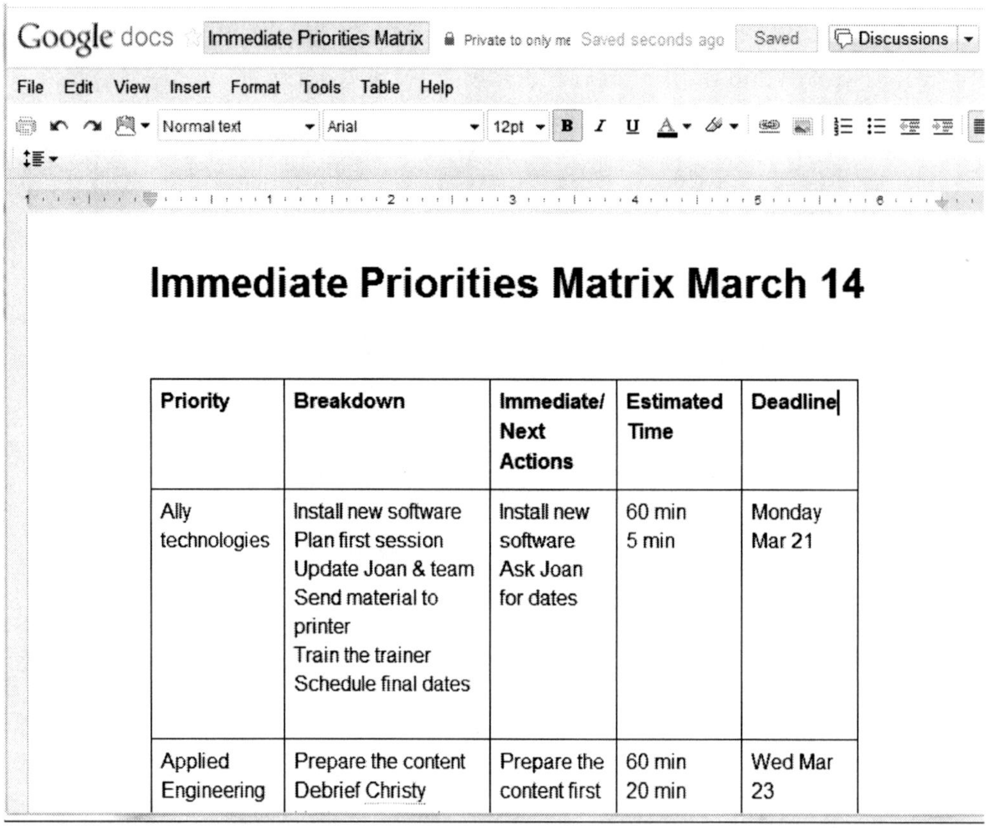

Immediate Priorities Matrix March 14

Priority	Breakdown	Immediate/ Next Actions	Estimated Time	Deadline
Ally technologies	Install new software Plan first session Update Joan & team Send material to printer Train the trainer Schedule final dates	Install new software Ask Joan for dates	60 min 5 min	Monday Mar 21
Applied Engineering	Prepare the content Debrief Christy	Prepare the content first	60 min 20 min	Wed Mar 23

Figure 3: Follow-up scheduled on the calendar

Exercise 1: Immediate Priorities Matrix™

Fill out the matrix below with your priorities as explained in this chapter and then proceed to reserve some time on your calendar for the activities that have important deadlines associated with them.

Table 9: Immediate Priorities Matrix™

Priority	Breakdown	Immediate/ Next Actions	Estimated Time	Deadline

Action Plan

Identify the action items that you would like to take as a result of what was covered in this chapter. Indicate the timeframe in which you plan on taking these actions. Then report on the actual date in which you implemented them and a brief note about the results.

Table 10: Action Plan

Practice/Technique	I will start implementing this on (date?)	Actual start date	Actual end date	Comment/Results
Preparing my Immediate Priorities Matrix™				
Scheduling important activities on my calendar				
Setting expectations and negotiate timelines as necessary				
Add your own item:				
Add your own item:				
Add your own item:				

Chapter 9: The Results You Want – align daily activities with long term goals

In the previous chapter, we discussed the Immediate Priorities Matrix™ as a rescue tool and a planning tool to help us manage conflicting demands, feel less overwhelmed and more in control, manage expectations and negotiate effectively with others. The matrix dealt primarily with the immediate (the now and up to two weeks from now). Now that we have a better handle on the immediate, it is time to turn our attention to the longer term, and make sure that our daily effort is adding up to more significant longer term results. In this chapter, we will be introducing yet another matrix, the End Results Matrix™ which unlike the Immediate Priorities Matrix™ is intended to focus on the next 3 to 6 months.

Defining the End Results

Turn to a new page in the journal and write down today's date, and what you want to accomplish today which is "managing results." Start the Capture Page to capture the myriad of items that come up during the day so they don't interrupt your flow. Then start the Notes pages to capture meeting notes. We are now ready to tackle the topic of conflicting priorities and how we can best manage them.

On the Notes Page, list 3 to 5 key results that you intend to achieve in the next 3 to 6 months. This is what Joan wrote down in her first pass:

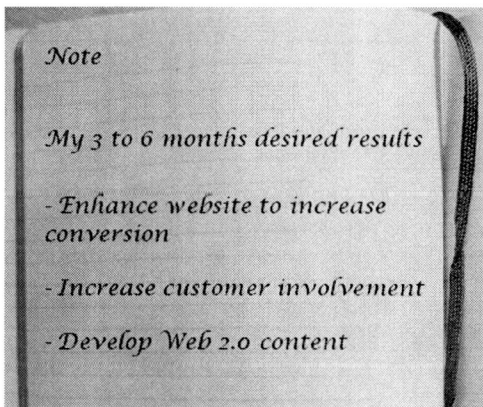

Figure 1: Desired results for next 3 to 6 months

Then as she thought through these results further, she started to be more specific. The more specific, more measurable, and attainable the results are the better. This is what the second pass looked like:

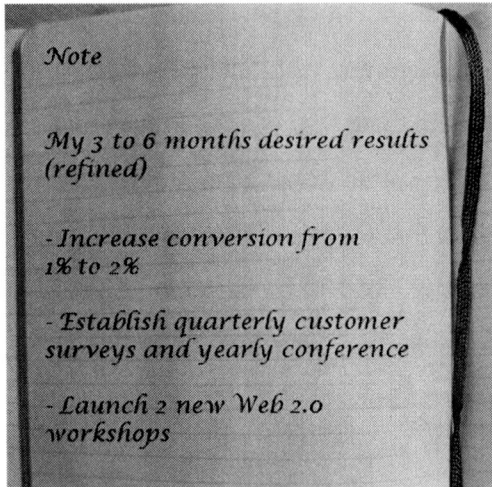

Figure 2: Results clarified

The End Results Matrix™

Once we have clarified the results that we are seeking in the next 3 to 6 months, the next step is to figure out the specific projects and activities that are necessary to create these results. This is the essence of what the End Results Matrix™ is about. Here is the format of the matrix:

Table 6: Sample End Results Matrix™

Result	Projects and tasks	Additional details

This is a sample end result detailed in the matrix:

Table 7: Sample result detailed in the matrix

Increase conversion from 1% to 2%	Enhance usability on website	Review website analytics Identify drop-off points Consult with a usability expert Redesign navigation Fill gaps in content Perform pilot test Implement remaining Web Pages

	Start loyalty program	Brainstorm with team Survey customers Get expert opinion Plan program
	Provide live support	Explore platforms Identify cost effective options Present plan to management

One of the valuable benefits of the End Results Matrix™ is that it prompts us to think through how we are going to get to our end results. It is the catalyst for strategic thinking and to planning the implementation details. These details may need to be further defined in other supporting documents as necessary.

The Immediate Priorities Matrix™ versus the End Results Matrix™

When you complete your End Results Matrix™, take a moment to compare it to your Immediate Priorities Matrix™. Go through the activities you have identified as immediate (and that are occupying your time and energy now and in the next two weeks) and compare them to the activities in the End Results Matrix™ and which are necessary for you to reach your 3 to 6 months results. What do you find when you compare these activities?

Most participants find that these activities do not match. They are out of sync. In other words, the kinds of activities that are keeping us busy on a daily basis, are not the same activities that are necessary for us to reach our long term results. What is the conclusion? Unfortunately, if we continue working this way, we will never reach the results we are hoping for. We end up disappointed, frustrated, and feeling not in control.

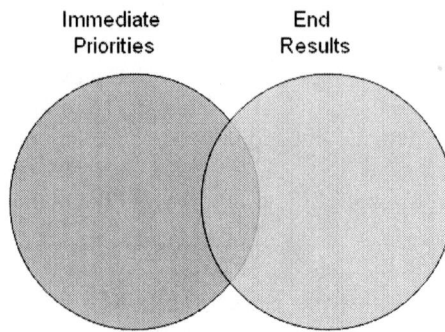

Figure 3: Misalignment between daily priorities and desired results

What we need is to align our daily activities with our long term results. This is probably one of the most crucial undertakings that we can possibly take and the most rewarding one. Here are some ideas on how this can be achieved.

From matrix to calendar again

In the previous chapter, we did the "matrix to calendar" exercise with our Immediate Priorities Matrix™ and it was intended for us to get a better handle on our competing priorities (and better manage expectations and negotiate resources and time when necessary). This time, we will do the "matrix to calendar" exercise for the End Results Matrix™. The goal is to schedule these activities (at least the initial ones that are necessary to get the related projects and initiatives started) on our calendar so they become reality.

The challenge we face most when we try to schedule such activities on our calendar is that our time is already fully scheduled for several weeks. It would be difficult if not impossible to add more activities to our calendar. The trick here is to look beyond the next few weeks and start to put these activities on our calendar for the future—maybe 2, 3, or even 4 weeks from now. Meanwhile, we can start to have informal conversations about these activities, get further buy-in from the stakeholders if necessary, start to work on setting expectations and negotiating resources and scope, and paving the road for success.

In one or two months, as we seriously engage in this alignment process, and bring more of our End Results Matrix™ activities to our calendar (and therefore to reality), our daily priorities are going to be more and more aligned with our end results:

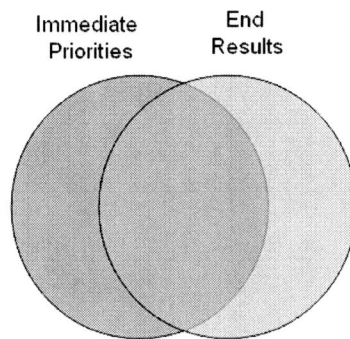

Figure 4: Priorities and results aligned

How often do we go back to these matrices?

As previously discussed, the Immediate Priorities Matrix™ is a tool that you can use on an as-needed basis or periodically such as every two weeks. The End Results Matrix™ on the other hand deals with 3 to 6 month periods and therefore it is likely that you would do it once every 3 to 6 months. The world is very dynamic however, and it continues to change unexpectedly and more frequently that we might desire. With these matrices in hand, we are always ready to respond to the change, and adjust as necessary.

Exercise 1: End Results Matrix™

Fill out the matrix below with your 3 to 5 key end results and the projects/tasks that will help you achieve these end results.

Table 8: End Results Matrix

Result	Projects and tasks	Additional details

Action Plan

Identify the action items that you would like to take as a result of what was covered in this chapter. Indicate the timeframe in which you plan on taking these actions. Then report on the actual date in which you implemented them and a brief note about the results.

Table 2: Action Plan

Practice/Technique	I will start implementing this on (date?)	Actual start date	Actual end date	Comment/Results
Prepare my End Results Matrix™				
Prepare supporting plans and relevant information				
Negotiate and get buy-in				
Schedule important tasks on my calendar				
Add your own item:				
Add your own item:				
Add your own item:				

Chapter 10: Information Sharing and Collaboration Using Google Docs, Google Sites, and Groups!

So you want an integrated system in the cloud. You got it! Google Apps is not just e-mail, chat, calendar, and tasks, but also documents, presentations, spreadsheets, forms and more, and all easily accessible from anywhere at any time[4]. These documents can also be shared with others and edited in real time by multiple users. Sharing information and co-creating become seamless. Let us get started!

Click on Documents which is one of the links on the top left, and then click on the "Create new" button to see the types of documents as shown below:

Figure 4: The Documents link gives you access to Google Docs

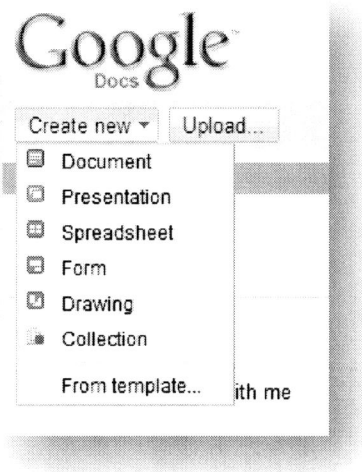

Figure 5: The types of documents you can create in Google Docs

---

[4] With Google Gear you can also access many of the Google Apps capabilities offline.

When you select the Document menu option, a blank document is created and ready for you to work on:

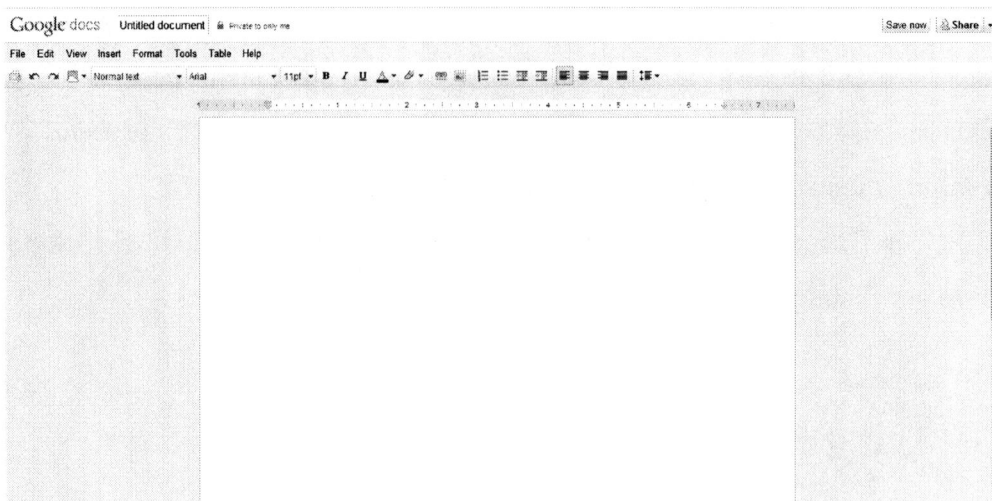

Figure 5: Newly created Google Docs document

In the remainder of this chapter, we will elaborate on what you can do with documents, and cover each of the document types (documents, presentations, spreadsheets, forms and more). For now, let us explore some of the common functionality and highlight important and useful aspects of Google Docs that you are likely to benefit from.

Cool Stuff You Want to Know About

Save Now

Google Docs documents are saved automatically and often. There is no need for you to explicitly save your documents. However you still have the option of saving using the Save Now button instead of waiting until the next automatic save to take place.

Share

Share allows you to share the document with others. The dropdown menu includes the following options:

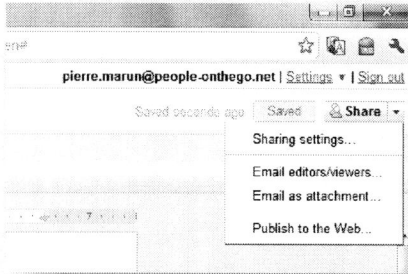

Figure 6: Sharing documents

The "Sharing settings" option allows you to indicate the e-mail addresses of the people that you want to share the document with, include a personal message to them, decide whether you want them to be able to edit or only view the document, and indicate how they will get notified about the sharing:

Figure 7: Sharing settings

Editing in Real Time

One of the unique features of Google Docs is allowing multiple users to edit the same document at the same time. This is the ultimate form of collaboration which I referred to earlier as "co-creating." Users can see each other's changes instantaneously. No need to take meeting notes and e-mail them later. The notes are created, seen, and shared right then. The meeting becomes a working session and the discussion becomes real work that results in immediate progress. Whether the context is brainstorming, planning, project management, reporting, or content creation, and whether users are in the same office or spread across continents. Everyone can leverage everyone else's ideas and create a group "memory" that helps engage people and facilitate follow-up activities.

Seeing Revision History

Google Docs allows you to see easily the revision history of a document:

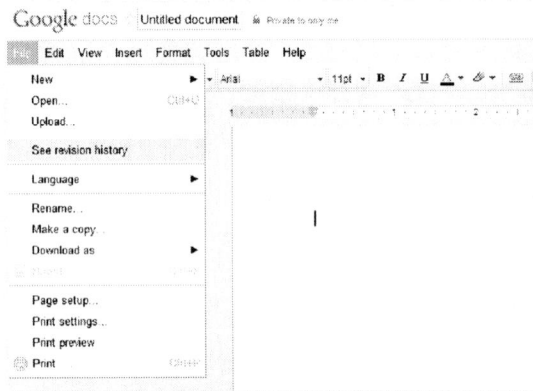

Figure 8: Seeing revision history

The revision history appears on the right side listing the revisions and allowing you to view the desired revision. This provides an audit trail and helps you and your team easily find out who changed what, and if necessary, restore a previous revision of the document.

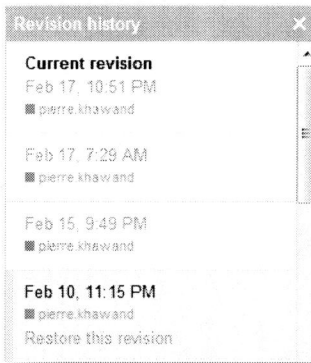

Figure 9: Revision history

Uploading and Downloading

Google Docs allows you to import existing documents that you have in any of the popular formats, and export documents that you create or edit in Google Docs to a variety of formats. This is what the upload screen looks like once you select Upload[5] from the File menu:

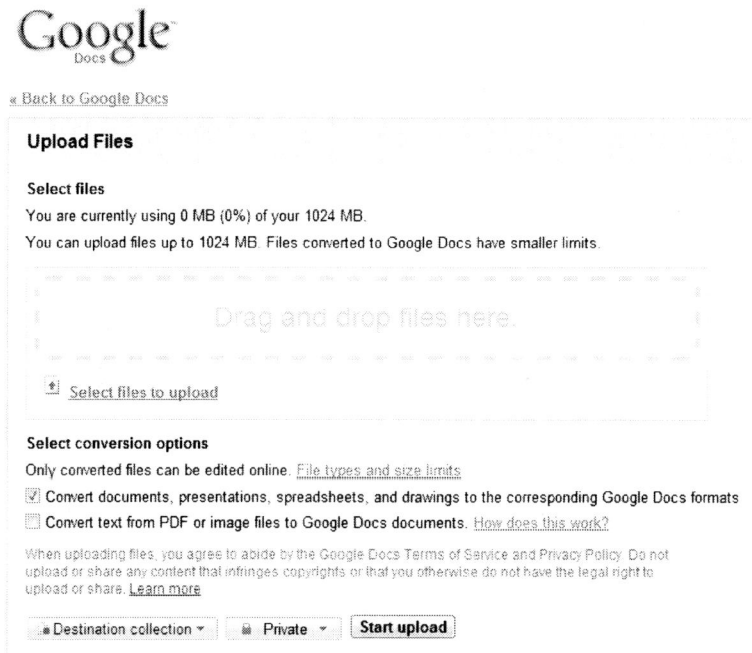

Figure 10: Uploading files into Google Docs

---

[5] The above screen show you the basic upload feature but you can also upload files and folders.

Google Collections

Collections are similar to folders in traditional file systems. A collection can have any number and variety of documents within it. You can easily create collections and then drag documents into your collections to organize your documents. You can create collections within your collections:

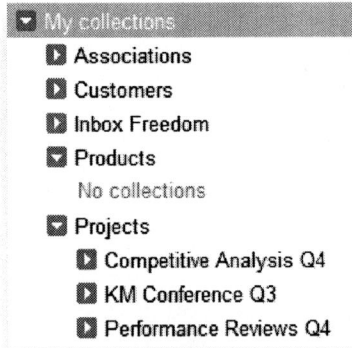

Figure 11: Collections illustrated

We mentioned earlier in the book that you can apply multiple labels to an e-mail message. Similarly, you can also apply multiple Collections to a document unlike a traditional folder system, which allows you to store a document in only one folder.

Viewing and managing documents

The Home view lists all documents and collections sorted in reverse chronological order (based on date last opened). However you can easily change the sort order using the "Sort by" drop down which allows you to sort by Priority, Title, and Last Modified.

Alternatively, you can display the starred items, all items, or the deleted items, by selecting Starred, All items, and Trash on the left. Or you can select the desired collection to view the items stored within this collection. There are also additional options that you can use such as the document type, images and videos, visibility, and ownership.

Once an item is selected such as a document or a collection, there are a number of actions that you can take on this item by clicking the Actions dropdown of the selected item:

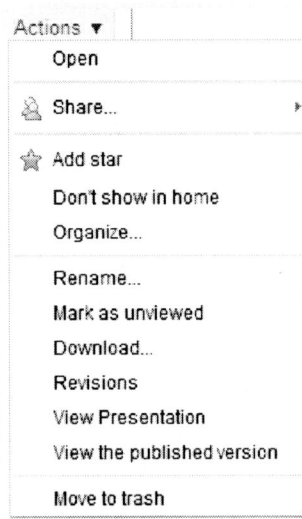

Figure 12: Actions that you can take on a document or collection

Documents

Let us go back to the document we created above and start to add the outline for our marketing plan (using this hypothetical marketing plan as an example) and then explore some of the capabilities in Google Docs that can help us give this document a professional look and feel, and make it user friendly:

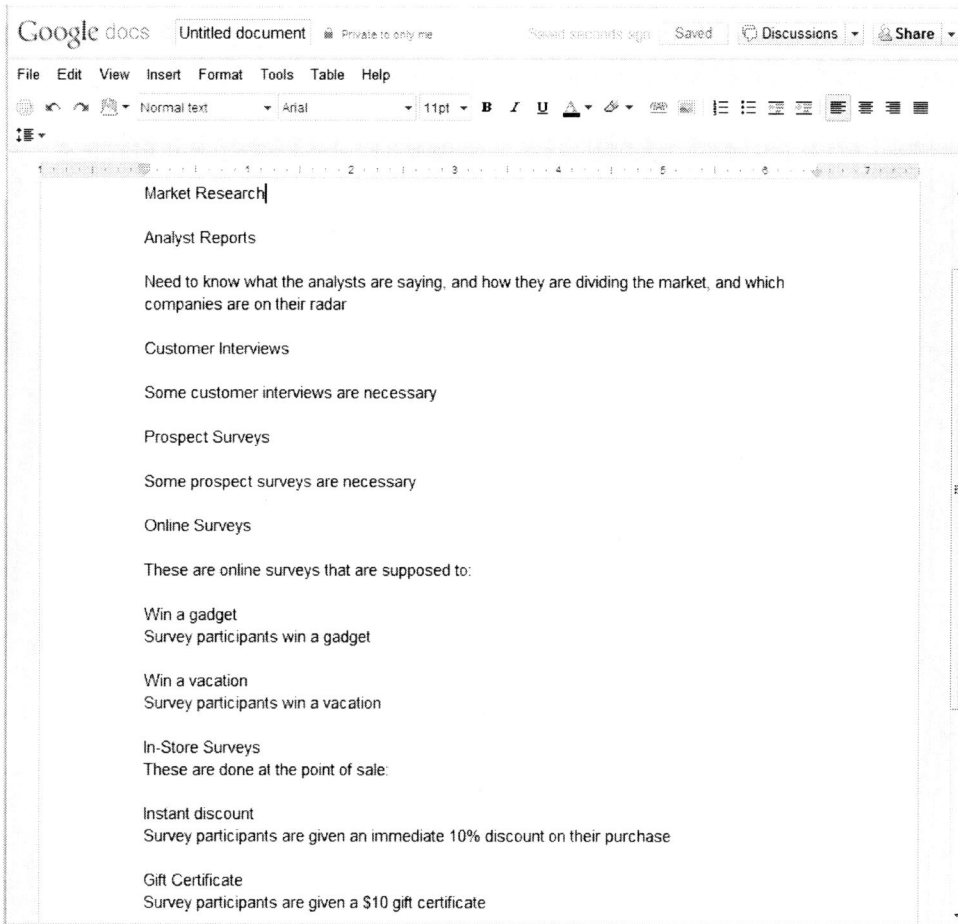

Figure 13: Marketing plan outline in a Google Docs document

Using styles

You can apply different styles to the text by selecting the appropriate text and then selecting the desired style from the dropdown on the toolbar (or from the Format menu, and then Paragraph Styles sub-menu):

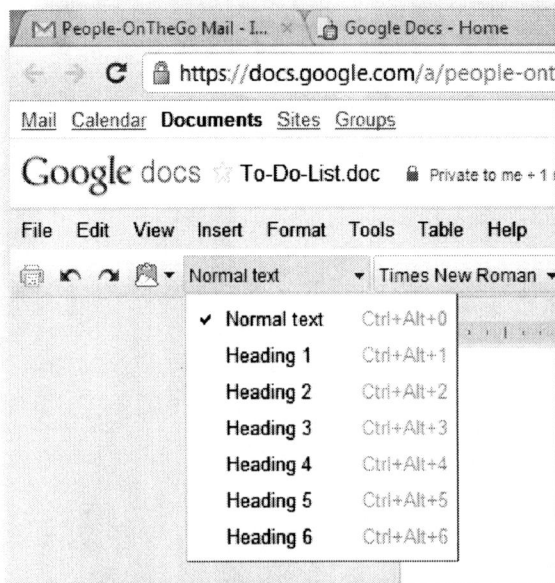

Figure 14: Assigning styles to the selected text in the document

Let us use Heading 1 to mark the main topics, and Heading 2 to market the next level topics, and then Heading 3, Heading 4, and so on. Using these styles makes our document easy to read and visually more appealing. Most importantly, it enables us to quickly create a table of contents based on these styles.

Below is a sample document showing the same content as above but using the styles we discussed:

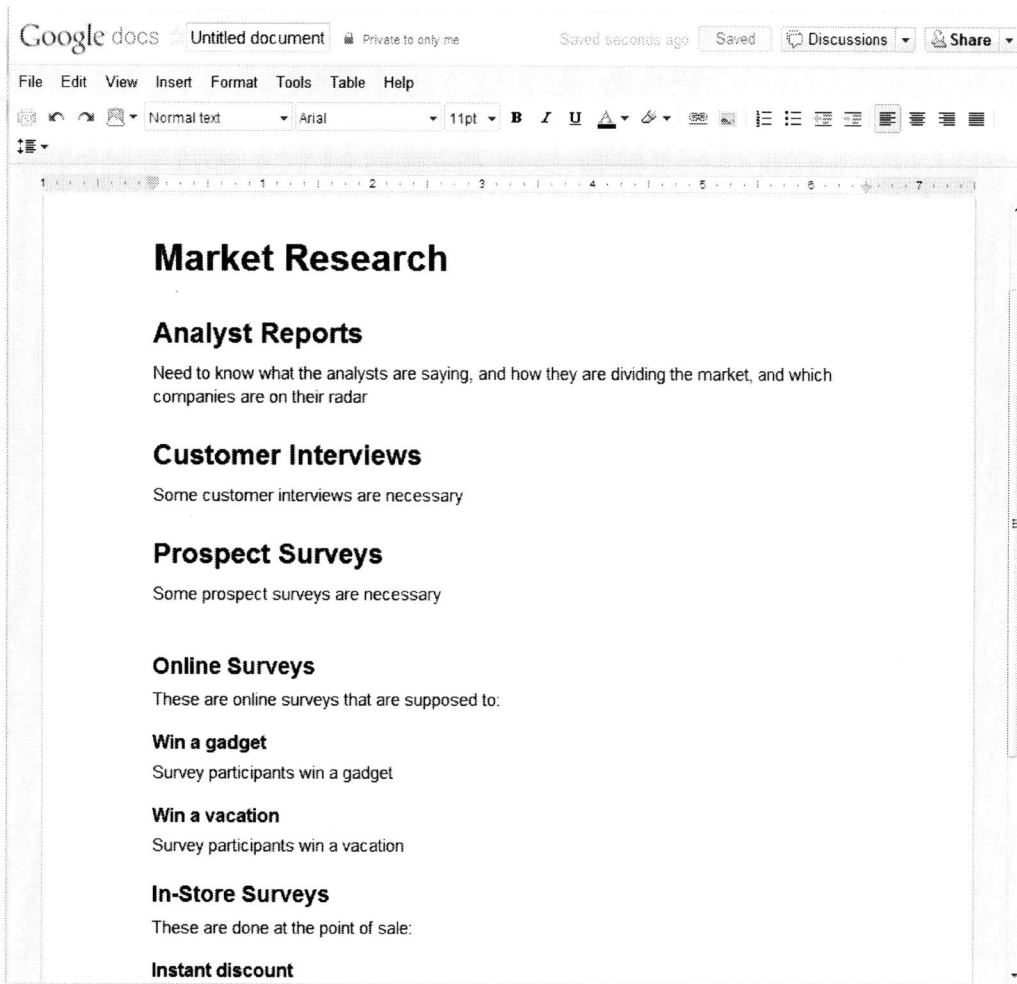

Figure 15: Marketing plan outline after assigning the headings styles

Creating a table of content

From the Insert menu, select "Table of contents" to insert a table of contents. Google Docs relies on the styles that were assigned above to create the table of contents. In addition, as the document evolves and more content is added, it is easy to update the table of contents by clicking the "Update now" button:

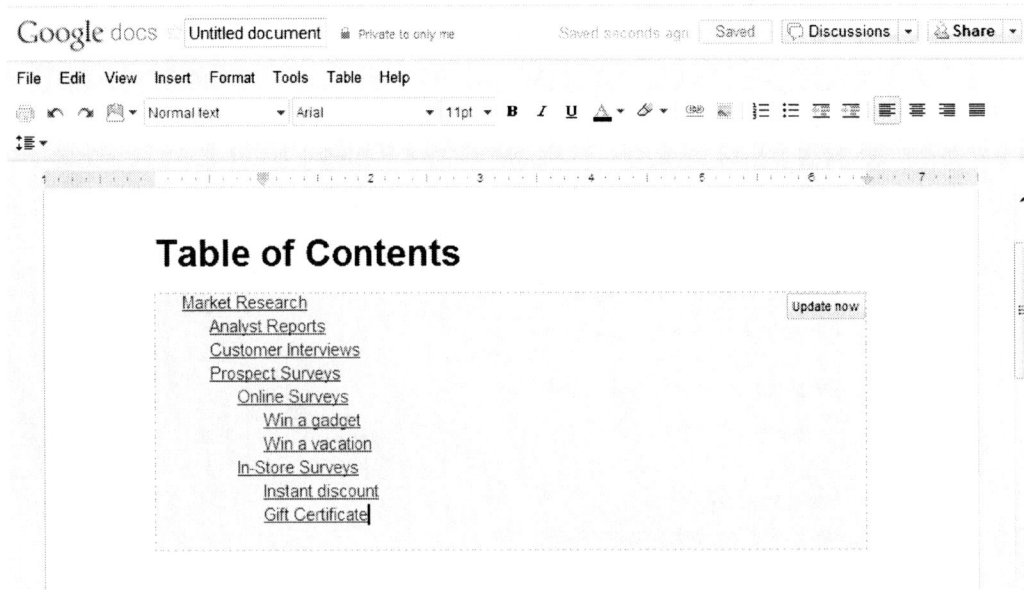

Figure 16: Marketing plan outline after assigning the headings styles

Clicking on one of the items in the table of contents allows you to go to the corresponding section in the document.

Remember the cool features we mentioned above

Let us say I would like to send this document to my colleagues so they can review it, give me feedback, and/or contribute to it. You know by now that in Google Docs we don't have to "send" documents. We just share them. We enable others to edit or to just view the documents. We can also work on these documents simultaneously with others and edit the documents in real time. At any point in time, we can review the revision history and easily see how the document evolved, who changed what, and even restore a previous revision.

And there is more!

Google Docs allows you to add images, links, drawings, comments, headers and footers, bookmarks and more as shown in the Insert menu below:

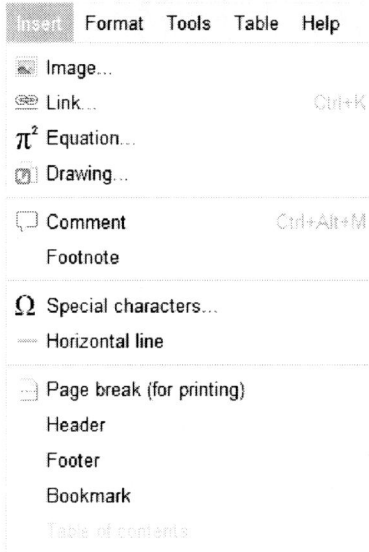

Figure 17: Assigning styles to the selected text in the document

And now moving to presentations to show you how you can create, edit, share, and embellish your presentations with Google Docs.

Presentations

As illustrated above, in addition to creating new presentations in Google Docs, you can upload existing presentations. For instance, this is a Microsoft PowerPoint presentation that was uploaded into Google Docs:

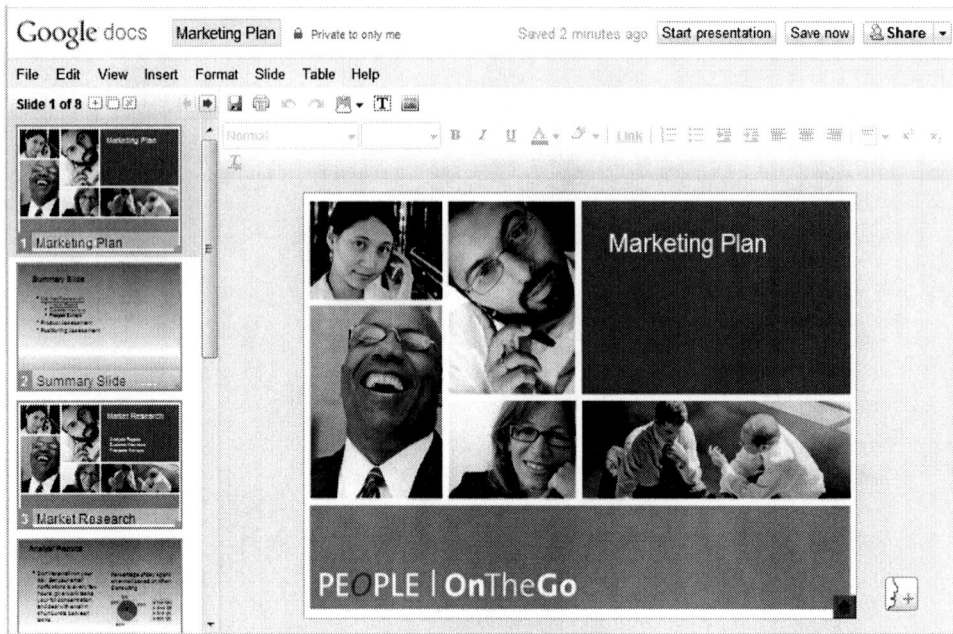

Figure 18: PowerPoint Presentation uploaded into Google Docs

From the View menu, you can choose to "Show speaker notes" to add speaker notes to your slides. The Insert menu allows you to insert text, images, drawings, videos, tables, and other shapes. The Format menu allows you to change your presentation settings including themes and backgrounds.

The Start Presentation button allows you to show the presentation to your audience, advance from one slide to the next, navigate to the desired slide, as well as print, download, and view with other users, among other things:

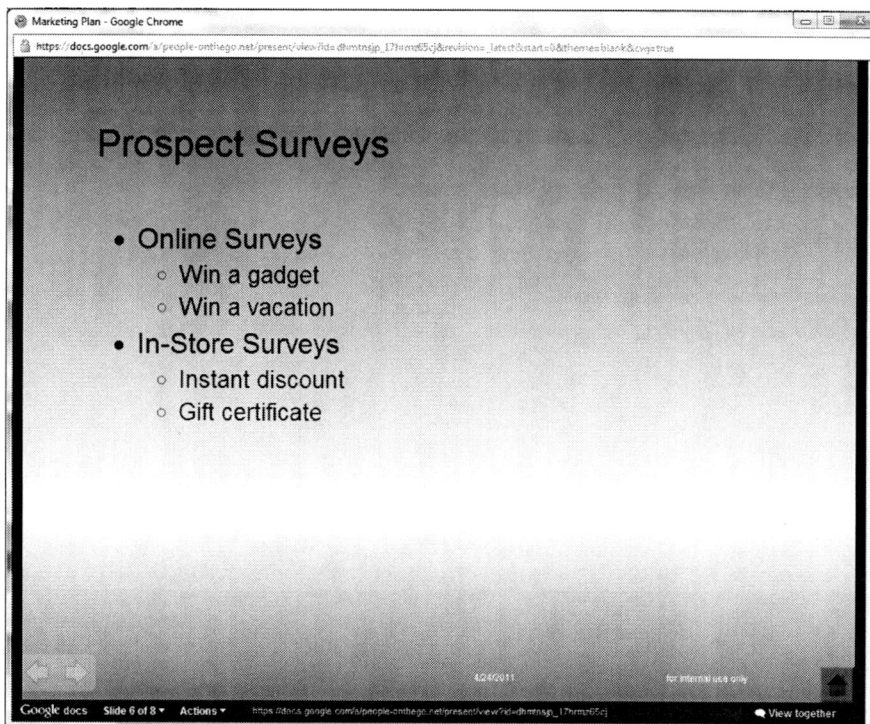

Figure 19: Start Presentation allows you to show your presentation to your audience

Remember the cool features we mentioned above

Let us say, I experience the "presenter's block" and I could use some help in creating my presentation. I know that one of my colleagues in our NYC office is very creative and always willing to help. I share my Google Docs presentation with her (as illustrated above) and check her chat status to see if she is focused or collaborative (see chapter 1 to learn more about these techniques). It happens to be my lucky day; she is in her collaboration session and therefore available to have live discussions. We switch to a voice chat, while we review the presentation together, and start a brainstorming session. Within minutes, ideas start to pour in and my presentation is right on track.

Spreadsheets

Let me create a new spreadsheet to track the registrations in our upcoming workshops. Click on the "Create new" button in the Google Docs screen and then select the spreadsheet option from the dropdown menu:

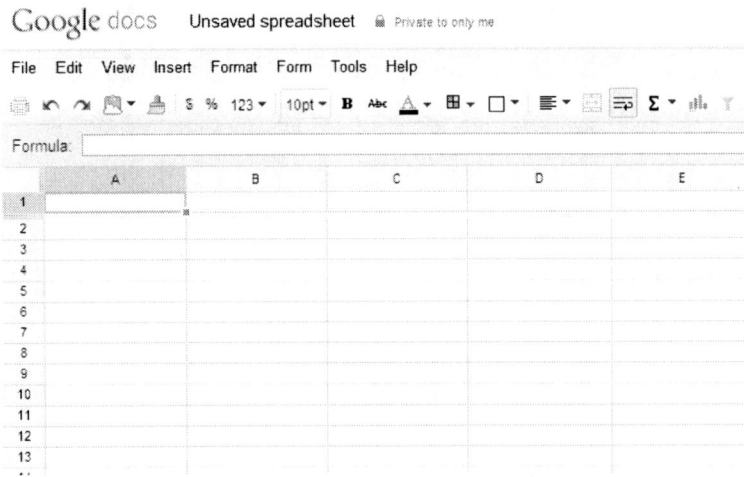

Figure 20: New spreadsheet in Google Docs

I would like to track the registrant name, the title of the workshop that the registrant registers for, as well as the location, date, and registration fee:

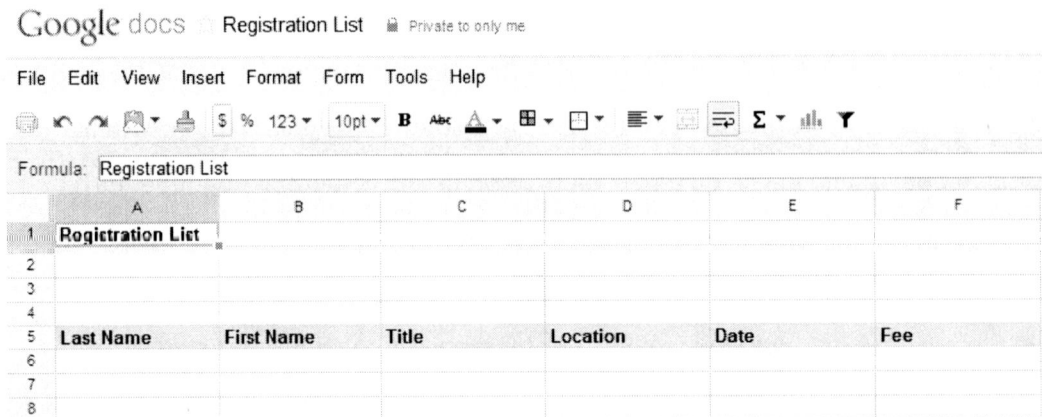

Figure 21: Registration List spreadsheet showing column headings for registration data

Let us see if we can make this registration spreadsheet easier to use and minimize data entry errors. Consider first the Title column in which our customer service team member enters the actual title of the workshop that the registrant would like to register for. For example, suppose that we are offering three workshops: Google Apps, Lotus Notes, and Microsoft Outlook. Obviously, the customer service team member can simply type the title of the desired workshop in the Title column; however there is a better way.

Select cell C6 and then from the Google Docs menu, select Tools, then Data Validation, then in the Criteria field, select "Items from a list", and then enter the desired items (in this case, the workshop titles):

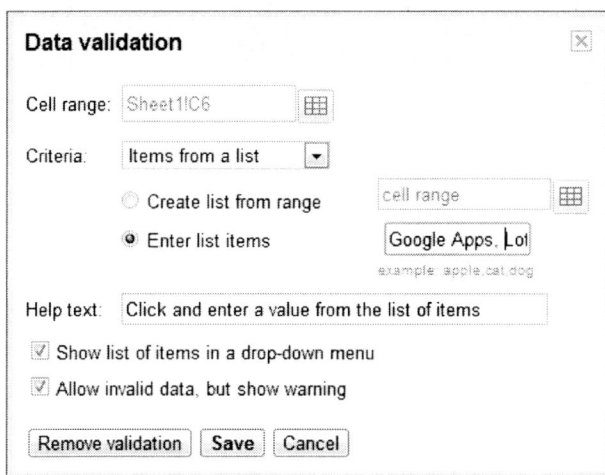

Figure 22: Data validation settings

Once I save the above settings, cell C6 turns into a dropdown that allows the customer service team member to select a value instead of typing one in:

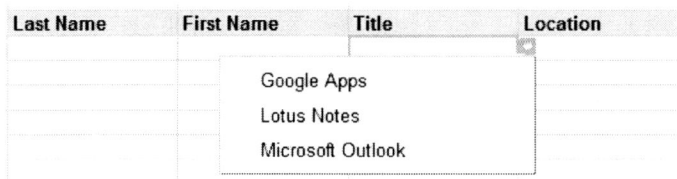

Figure 23: Selecting an item from a list instead of having to type the value in

As we continue our journey of making this spreadsheet easier to use and less prone to error, we also want to create a list of workshop locations so we don't have to enter these manually for each registration. Knowing that we have many locations and that we are likely to be adding new locations along the way, instead of entering the list in the Data Validation window, I would like to have this list in a new sheet and refer to the list. I create a new sheet, enter the list of locations, then add the data validation as illustrated below:

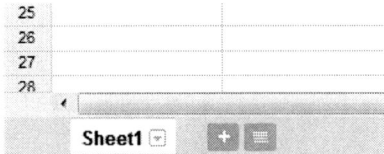

Figure 24: Clicking on the + sign (lower left corner) to create a new sheet

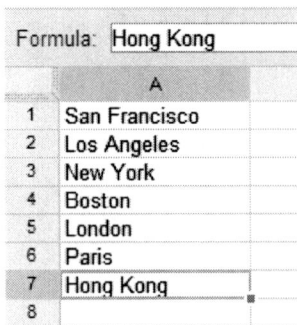

Figure 25: Entering the locations list in Sheet 2

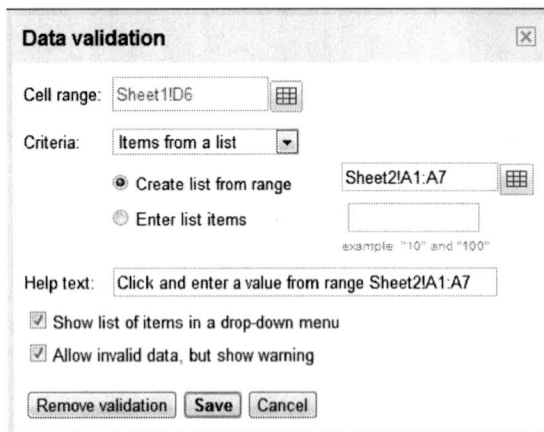

Figure 26: Selecting "Create list from range" and indicating the range

---

For the Date column in my registration list, I also add a data validation to ensure that the date entered is a valid date. I select cell E6, then select Tools from the menu, then Data Validation, and select Date in the Criteria field:

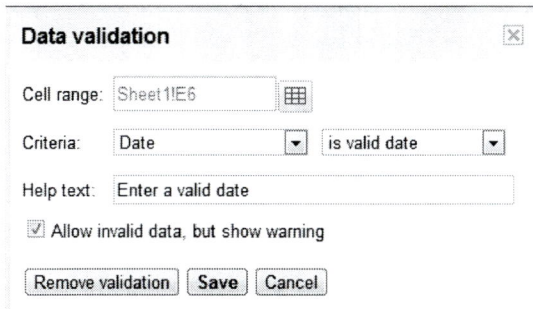

Figure 27: Adding a data validation for the workshop dates

And finally, for the fee (cell F6), I add a data validation to ensure that the fee entered is between $0 and $500:

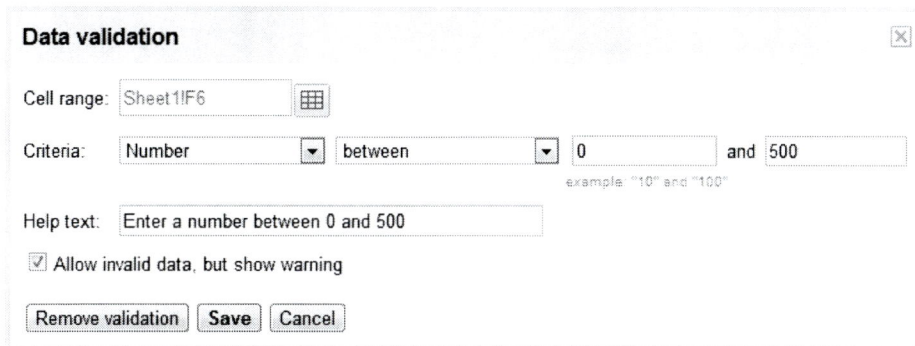

Figure 28: Adding a data validation for the workshop registration fee

Now that I have these data validation settings in cells C6 to F6, how do I extend them to the cells below? This is actually easy using the "copy" and "paste format only" commands. You select cells C6 to F6 and then copy these cells (by selecting Copy from the Edit menu, or using the keyboard shortcut Ctrl+C), and then select the desired cells where you want the format to be copied (such as C7 to F30) and then select the "paste formats only" menu item from the Edit menu.

There is a lot more that you could explore in Google Docs spreadsheets. The above gave you a head start in making your spreadsheets user friendly!

Forms

Creating a form

Google forms allow you to create web forms, collect data, and view responses quickly and easily. Once upon a time this process required the involvement of web designers and programmers and a whole chain of people who needed to approve it. If approved, and after weeks of wait time and back and forth exchanges, you might get something that resembles what you wanted. No more!

Creating a form, similar to creating a document, a presentation, or a spreadsheet, starts with the Create new dropdown by selecting Form:

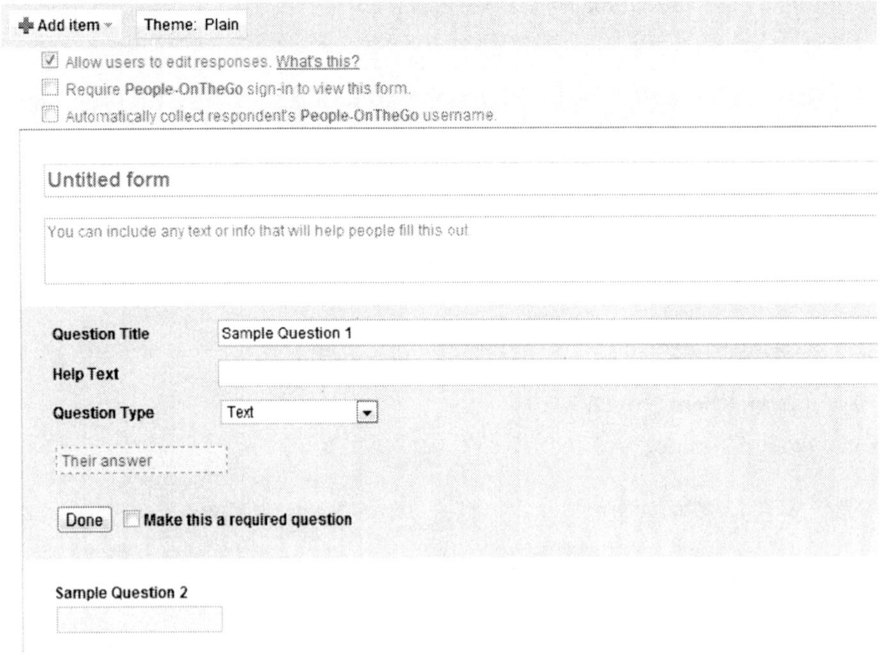

Figure 29: Creating forms in Google Docs

Google Docs allow you to create forms for internal use only or for broader distribution. You can set these and more options as you create your form as shown in the form above. You can also set a theme for your form. Below is a sample form we created to poll our users about which e-mail client they are using, and if they are using Gmail, which is their favorite Labs:

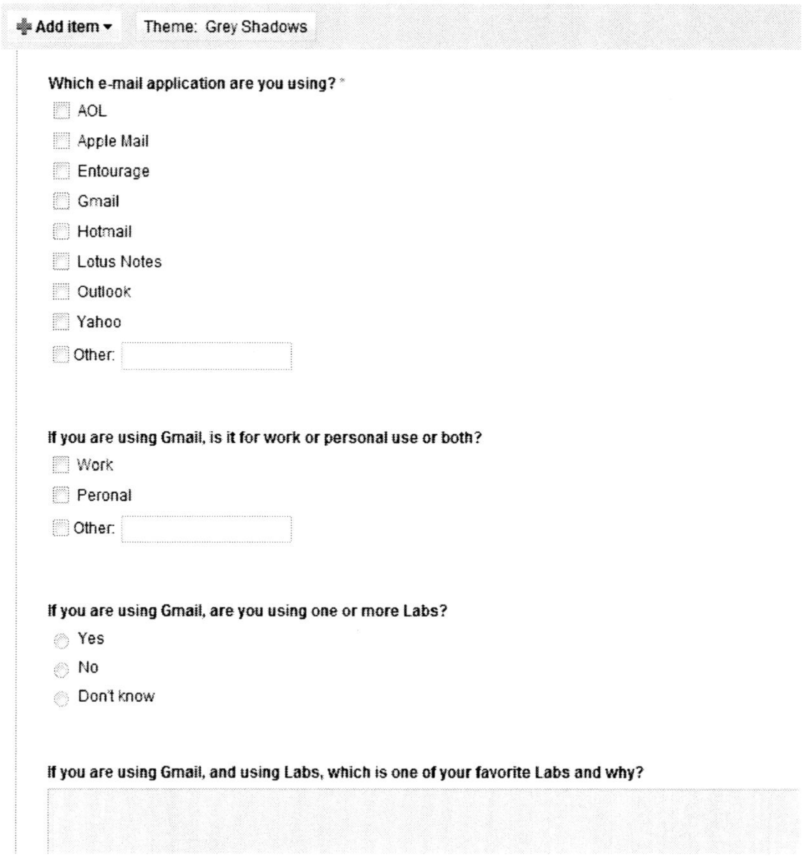

Figure 30: Sample Google Docs form with a variety of question types

Managing the Google Docs form

Once you create the form, you can email it to your audience to collect responses, and then see the responses. The buttons on the top left allow you to manage the form easily and provide several options:

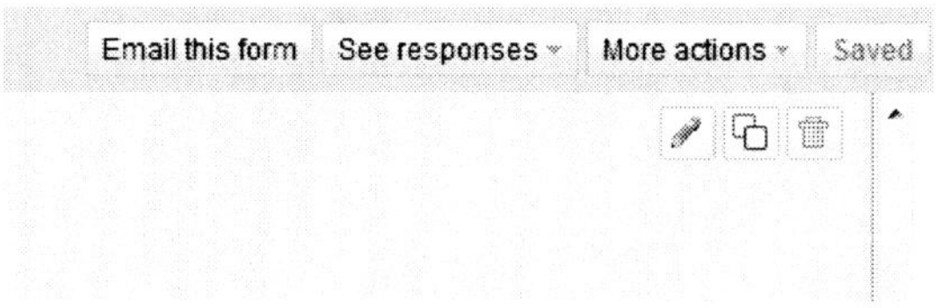

Figure 31: Managing the Google Docs form

The responses are collected in a Google Docs spreadsheet which allows you to easily review them at any time.

Sites

Click on Sites which is one of the links on the top left in Google Apps in order to access Sites, then click on "Create new site" to create a new site as shown below:

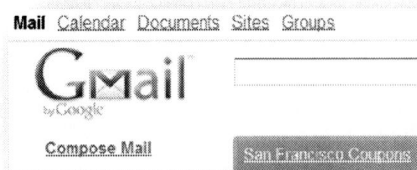

Figure 32: The Sites link gives you access to Sites

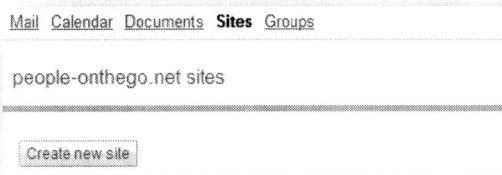

Figure 33: Creating a new site

Figure 34: New site settings

Sites that you create in Google Apps can be internal and available only to users in your domain, shared with outside users, or even made public. These settings are initially set by the Google Apps administrator at your organization and then users can then share sites accordingly.

This is the site we created which is now ready to be populated with content. All internal users can access the site and post information. This is the ultimate collaboration platform where everyone can contribute at any time and everyone else can leverage everyone else's ideas:

Figure 35: New site created in Google Apps using one of the existing templates

Editing pages on the site

This is easy to do and it starts by selecting the Edit page button on the top right:

Figure 36: Editing pages

The Insert menu and the formatting toolbar allows you to add a variety of objects to the page and format the content:

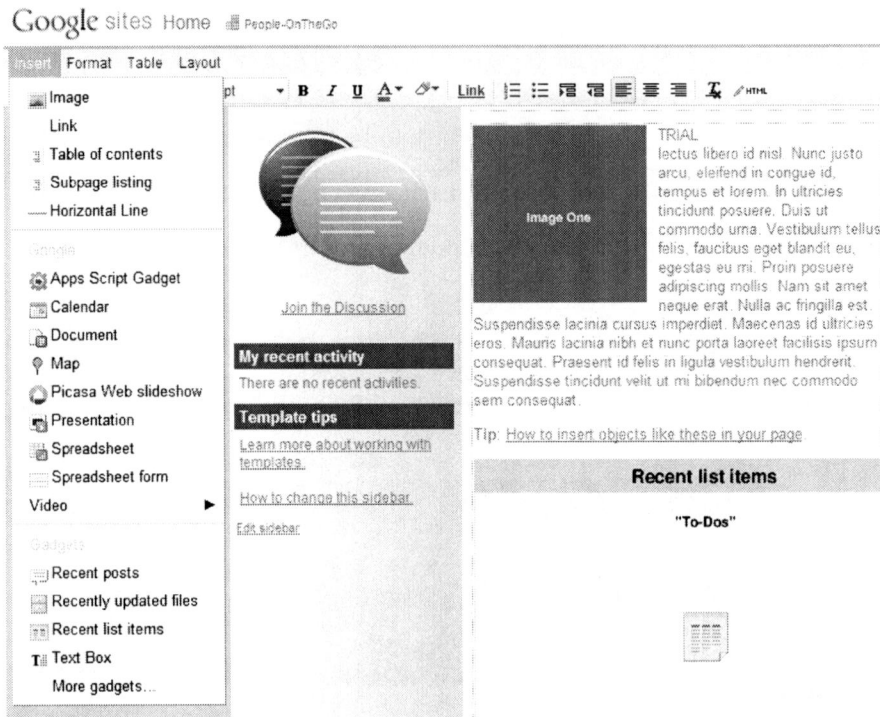

Figure 37: Inserting a variety of objects on a page

And there is always more!

This chapter provided some insights into how Google Apps provide an integrated environment for managing documents and collaborating seamlessly with others internally and externally. We demonstrated some key concepts and features in most of the applications, but there is much more to Google Apps, from being able to create drawings, to creating and managing groups and making communication easier, and much more. Let the learning continue!

Action Plan

Identify the action items that you would like to take as a result of what was covered in this chapter. Indicate the timeframe in which you plan on taking these actions. Then report on the actual date in which you implemented them and a brief note about the results.

Table 4: Action Plan

Practice/Technique	I will start implementing this on (date?)	Actual start date	Actual end date	Comment/Results
Using documents				
Using spreadsheets				
Using presentations				
Create a form to survey my team				
Creating an external form to survey my customers or partners				
Create a site for internal collaboration				
Add your own item:				
Add your own item:				
Add your own item:				

Chapter 11: The De-stress Secrets—manage stress before it manages you

Turn to a new page in the journal and write down today's date, and what you want to accomplish today which is "manage stress." Start the Capture Page and the Notes page. We are now ready to tackle the topic of managing stress in the workplace. Let us start with this exercise which you can do on the Notes page. Fill in the blank in this sentence:

Stress is when_____

Go ahead, take a few minutes and jot down the various situations that cause you to be stressed. Write down as many as you can.

When we ask our workshop participants to do this exercise, we get items such as:

Stress is…

- when I am asked to do more things than what I have time for
- When priorities keep changing on me
- When my colleagues don't deliver what they promised and therefore I cannot get my tasks completed
- When I am not able to do a great job because of factors that are outside my control
- When I don't know the answer
- When I am held responsible for something I have not done
- When I have difficult people to deal with
- and many more!

I would like to suggest that all of the above situations, and probably the ones that you have written down in your journal, are likely to fall in the following categories:

➢ Unfinished/unresolved items lurking in the background
➢ People who (or things that) are not the way that we want them to be
➢ Being overly concerned about what happened in the past or might happen in the future

In the rest of this chapter, we will explore three primary techniques that can help us better manage the above situations. If you practice these techniques, you are likely to reduce stress significantly. The goal here is not to eliminate stress (which is not desired because some level of stress is healthy and can be quite motivating), but to contain it, manage it well, and get it to work for you instead of against you. As you start to manage stress effectively, the energy that has been taken over by stress will be released and your accomplishments are likely to multiply. Your ability to focus and collaborate will increase dramatically and most importantly, you feed good, or even great, and sometimes ecstatic.

First Technique: The Awareness Wheel

The Awareness Wheel, a technique that was originally described by Sherod & Phyllis Miller (authors of "Core Communication, Skills and Processes") can help us take a difficult situation, break it down into more manageable components and identify how best to handle it. The pre-requisite to using the Awareness Wheel is to clearly define the difficult situation or issue. Clearly defining the situation is an important first step in this process. When the situation is not clearly defined, it is especially difficult to work with. It would be like chasing a ghost.

Then the next step would be to break down this seemingly difficult situation into five components which are presented in the five sections of the wheel below.

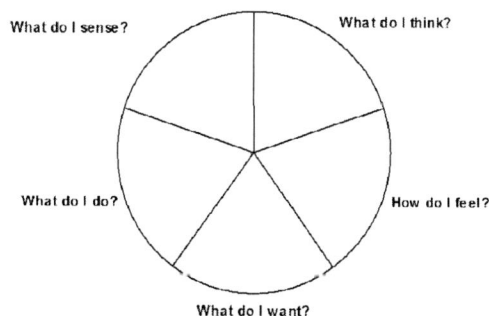

Figure 1: Awareness Wheel

Let us walk through each of these components.

Each component presents a question that you need to answer to the best of your ability. These questions prompt us to think more thoroughly about the situation and identify what is truly going on so we can be in a better position to manage the situation. Below are the questions and what they mean.

1. What do I sense about the situation? We have five senses that give us specific data about the environment we live in. The point here is to identify what this data is such as what did I see and what did I hear.

2. What do I think about the situation? This has to do with what is going on in our mind. And a lot is usually going on in our mind. These range from interpretations, to opinions, to conclusions, and a lot more.

3. How do I feel about the situation? Examples may be sadness, anger, or fear on one side, and joy, and happiness, on the other side, and all shades in between.

4. What do I want in this situation? This has to do with being more aware of our wants, and as we go through the wheel, becoming more aware of our real wants (as opposed to the initial reactionary wants).

5. What do I do in this situation? This has to do with identifying the potential actions and ideally the best possible action.

In a perfect world, we would be able to run through these questions one by one, become more aware of what is really going on, and be in a better position to identify and take the appropriate action. In the real world however, the complexity of the human mind and emotions, and the interdependence between thoughts and feelings, wants and actions, we are likely to go through this multiple times (hence the concept of a wheel) and not necessarily in order. The case study below illustrates how the Awareness Wheel can be applied to help better manage a difficult situation.

The case study

Mark is unhappy at work and when asked to define the problem, here is how he put it: "My boss doesn't care about my professional development and I am really unhappy at work." This situation is very stressful for Mark and is taking up a lot of his energy. His working relationships are impacted, he is not feeling good at work and even outside work, and his performance is suffering. Let us see how the Awareness Wheel can help. We will demonstrate how a coach can help Mark use the Awareness Wheel to manage this situation:

Coach: "Mark, what happened?"

Mark: "She doesn't care"

Where does Mark's statement ("She doesn't care") fall in the Awareness Wheel? This is Mark's subjective view of what happened. This is clearly his interpretation of what happened. It is a thought. The coach makes a note of this in the Awareness Wheel, indicating to Mark that this is his interpretation, and repeats the question again:

Coach: "Tell me more about what actually happened?"

Mark: "She cancelled the meeting"

This is a fact. Mark reports real data. He *saw* (with his "senses") the meeting cancelled notice in his e-mail inbox. The coach takes note of this and proceeds to help Mark explore the feeling part:

Coach: "Mark, how do you feel about the meeting being cancelled?"

Mark: "I feel I am not important"

Even though Mark uses the words "I feel," the statement "I am not important" is more of an interpretation than a feeling. Using words such as "I feel" to express a thought is common. There might be a feeling associated with the thought, but that is something that would need to be explored. For now, the "I am not important" statement is noted as a thought. Now the coach tries to get to the feeling behind the thought.

Coach: "Mark, how else are you feeling about this?"

Mark pauses for a bit and then says: "I am sad and disappointed"

As you may have noticed already, the coach tends to repeat the same question more than once. The first time, he usually gets a reactionary answer such as "I feel that I am not important" and then the second time (or sometime third or fourth time) he gets more meaningful insights into what is really going on such as "I am sad and disappointed."

The coach continues to explore this area with Mark, and then when he thinks that Mark is ready to move to the next component, the coach makes an initial attempt at asking Mark about his wants.

Coach: "So what do you want Mark"

Mark: "I want to have the meeting"

Then Mark proceeds to say:

Mark: "I will tell her that I am unhappy."

Mark has just expressed an action here (not necessary the best action, but it is an action). The Coach notices that the want and action expressed by Mark are reactionary, so he asks Mark again about his thoughts and feelings about the situation, and gives him the opportunity to express these further and spend time exploring these. Then later in the conversation, the coach makes another attempt at asking Mark about what Mark really wants. Mark takes a deep breath at that point, and says:

Mark: "I want more recognition."

Then Mark adds: "I want input on my career development."

This is a big "Ah-Ha" moment for Mark! Mark just realized it is not the meeting that really got him emotionally mixed up and stressed, it is the underlying need to have recognition and the desire for a better career development plan that he seems to be missing at work. The meeting was just the tip of the iceberg and his reaction to the meeting being cancelled is just that, a reaction. This is one of the key purposes of the wheel – to facilitate the process of becoming more aware of the real causes behind what we are experiencing on the surface.

Occasionally, workshop participants indicate that Mark should have easily realized that it was not the meeting that was causing his stress ("what is the big deal about a meeting being cancelled anyway"), and that it should have been clear to him that the lack of recognition and lack of career development opportunities were the real issues. When we talk to these participants further about the issues that are causing "them" stress, we find out that their issues are not more severe or different in nature from Mark's issues, and yet, these participants seem to get significantly stressed and emotionally involved when it comes to their own issues. So how does it happen that we have more clarity when it comes to other people's issues, and suddenly lose this clarity when it comes to our own issues?

This is largely because when we are experiencing the issues ourselves, we are "under their influence", emotionally involved in them, and therefore our judgment gets impaired. Yes indeed. Our Judgment gets impaired. At this point, when it gets impaired, even the smartest of us become unable (truly unable) to make the slightest distinction between data, opinions, feelings, and wants. Our emotions and deep seated fears take over. So while Mark's situation may seem easy to someone looking at it from the outside, maybe someone who hasn't experienced a similar situation, it doesn't look that way for Mark, and probably for anyone who has experienced a similar situation.

In order to truly experience the Awareness Wheel, better understand it and see its usefulness, you need to apply it to a real situation that is causing you significant stress, substantial confusion, and inability to manage the situation effectively – a situation where your judgment is impaired. If you cannot think of such a situation, the Awareness Wheel and underlying concepts are likely to be helpful in better understanding and dealing with others who are experiencing these situations.

Back to Mark, the coach is now ready to ask the important question:

Coach: "So what are you going to do about this situation Mark?"

Mark: "I will ask to reschedule the meeting and discuss the real issues with my boss"

Then Mark adds: "I will also find a coach or a mentor"

Another big "Ah-Ha"!

The Awareness Wheel helped transform this difficult situation (or even seemingly insurmountable situation in Mark's mind at the time when his judgment is impaired) into an actionable one. We started with "My boss doesn't care about my professional development and I am really unhappy at work" and ended up with a better understanding of the underlying needs and specific action items that can be carried out in order to get these underlying needs met. Nicely done!

The job is not done however. Mark still needs to implement these actions. As he implements the actions, he needs to watch for his interpretations and assumptions sneaking in again. If he continues practicing the Awareness Wheel each step of the way, he will continue to refine and enhance his actions. Soon he will become experienced at this tool and use it more naturally to help him through difficult situations. He is now on his way to discovering a whole new world of accomplishments.

The purpose of the wheel

To start with, the simple act of defining the "issue" and getting engaged with the Awareness Wheel is in and by itself an empowering exercise. It puts our energy and creativity in motion. It helps us challenge the status quo and get busy with solutions – all essential to solving problems and feeling better. In addition, the Awareness Wheel serves several important and clear purposes:

1. It help us separate reality from imagination (events from interpretations)

2. It help us separate thoughts from feelings (what the mind is creating, as opposed to how we are truly feeling)

3. It help us identify our true wants (instead of our reactionary wants)

4. It facilitates identifying the best possible action

5. It enables us to positively influence our end results

In our daily work and personal life, the default sequence of events is that an event takes place in our environment for instance. we sense something (someone says or does something), we quickly interpret it in a certain way (unfortunately this may be the not-so-constructive way), we feel a certain way about it (not so positive feelings caused by not-so-constructive interpretations), and then act accordingly (poor action caused by this sequence). This whole sequence happens very quickly and transparently. We don't even notice it. It looks and feels as if we are just taking actions to deal with what happened, yet we wonder why we aren't getting the results we desire. The Awareness Wheel enables us to interfere and change this sequence. The end goal is significantly improved actions and results, not to mention breakthroughs!

Exhaust your creative thinking and problem solving skills

While there are certain difficult situations that we cannot do anything about, more often than not, it is possible to come up with plausible actions that we can take. This is exactly where creative thinking and problem solving come into play. This is where we want to go beyond the obvious, do our research, brainstorm with others, and uncover new possibilities.

It is difficult to get to the creative thinking and problem solving stage if we are stuck in our biased interpretations, negative feelings, and rigid wants. The Awareness Wheel can help us release these interpretations, feelings, and wants, and therefore go beyond them and apply our time and energy into formulating constructive actions.

So what if there is nothing we can do about the situation?

What if we go through the Awareness Wheel, exhaust our creative thinking and problem solving capabilities, and still conclude that there isn't much that we can do about the situation. If this is the case, it would be beneficial for us to stop banging our head against this situation and move on to better things – where our effort is fruitful and rewarding. The Awareness Wheel helps us make that determination faster and reach the acceptance stage sooner. Once we reach the acceptance stage, I would even suggest creating a "closed issues" category in the catch-all to-do list and adding the issue to that category so that our mind doesn't keep resurrecting the "closed" issue and wasting valuable energy.

Self-Coaching

We presented the case study above by having a coach walk through the Awareness Wheel with Mark. While it would be ideal to have a coach help us along the way, more often than not, we need to be our own coach. The Awareness Wheel is the ideal tool for self-coaching.

The Awareness Wheel components and related questions are exactly the kind of questions we should ask ourselves. Writing down the answers, as we progress through the process, is critical. This helps us avoid "spinning our wheels" by reiterating the same thoughts and feelings endlessly. This will also help us detect "imbalance" (spending too much time and energy on one component of the wheel without paying enough attention to the rest). The Awareness Wheel is largely about balance. It helps bring to the forefront all aspects of a situation. It helps us have a more objective view of the world as opposed to getting too focused on one area and losing ourselves in it.

As we saw in the case study, it is important to repeat the same question more than once to get beyond the initial superficial answer. It usually takes several passes to get to the core issues. If you don't get to the desired results in one session, you may want to give yourself a break, let the issues percolate, and then resume later. This process of self-questioning and self-coaching is one of the most worthwhile activities we can undertake if we want to succeed and feel better – accomplish more with less stress.

Coaching each other

Be careful! When it comes to coaching others to use the Awareness Wheel, things can get tricky. It is most tricky if you are in the midst of a conflict situation or a heated discussion with the other person. It is tempting at that time to want to share the Awareness Wheel techniques with the other party to help solve the situation. Your good intentions may not generate the desired results because the other party may not be open to coaching especially not in this setting.

However if you have already built some trust with the other party and shared the Awareness Wheel techniques ahead of time, and both agree that it would be beneficial to help each other through it when necessary, things can be much more promising.

And in situations where it is not possible or appropriate to share the Awareness Wheel and coach each other, one can still keep the Awareness Wheel handy and apply the techniques to help the situation. Using the Awareness Wheel should not depend on the other party and does not need to be a formal exercise. It can help us better understand what is going on for us, and potentially for the other party, and have a more effective interaction as a result.

For instance, it is far more empowering and effective to say "I saw that you cancelled this meeting" (the senses) and "my interpretation was that this issue is not important to you right now" (the thought), and "I felt nervous" (feeling), and then continue to say "I would like to make sure we move this issue forward and not run into potential project delays later" (want), and "what do you think we can do to address this situation?" (request for action in the form of a question). This is common sense and mature communication that can be achieved by practicing the Awareness Wheel and applying it genuinely to everyday situations.

Second Technique: Rational Thinking

The Rational Emotive Theory which was pioneered by Dr. Albert Ellis, the author of "How to stubbornly refuse to make yourself miserable about anything – yes anything" has some valuable insights to offer when it comes to managing stress.

When we are overly stressed about a situation, it is very likely that we have an irrational (unrealistic) believe about the situation that is causing the extra stress, more so than the situation itself. This is common sense and commonly forgotten. The situation itself may call for some caution, and may be uncomfortable, or even stressful, but it is the underlying belief that is likely to be causing the "overly" stressful perception and the thoughts and feelings that "we cannot stand it."

If we uncover this underlying irrational belief, and work at replacing it with a more rational (realistic) belief, then it is likely that at the minimum we will be a lot less stressed, and at best, we may even be in a position to take more constructive actions and influence the situation positively.

The case study

Mark is overly stressed and almost panicky when John doesn't turn in his status report on time. Mark cannot stand the situation, he's angry, and he cannot stand John when this happens. This is affecting his working relationship with John and his ability to come up with a workable solution for this issue. This is also affecting his feeling about his work, his team, and the whole organization that allows someone like John to get away with this behavior.

What is the underlying irrational belief(s) behind Mark's problem? We can probably identify several of them – depending on how deep we want to go with our analysis. However, for the sake of our case study, let us stick to these two:

1. People "should" give their status reports on time

2. "I cannot stand it" when they don't give their status report on time

Well, let us examine these beliefs further. They are both unrealistic. They don't conform to reality. Beliefs that don't conform to reality are likely to bring us frustration and stress. The first belief includes a strong "should." Whenever we hold on to beliefs that are loaded with strong "shoulds", we are asking for trouble. Who said or guaranteed us that people "should" give their status reports on time? No one ever did. This belief is not real. The proof that this belief is not real is that people aren't giving their status reports on time. If it was such a given that people "should" give their status report on time, then they would. But in reality some of them don't, and therefore this "should" is unrealistic. The second belief includes another unrealistic statement: "I cannot stand it when___." In reality Mark is standing it. He hasn't vanished and life is still going on.

So what would be the more rational beliefs that could replace the irrational ones mentioned above? How about: "It is frustrating when John doesn't give his status report on time, however even though it is inconvenient and not ideal, I can stand it and I can manage it." This is reality!

Working at replacing initial beliefs that are rigid and unrealistic with the second one, which is flexible and realistic, is likely to cause the following:

1. Mark will feel better. By simply thinking about the situation differently, he is going to feel less stressed about it.

2. With the new attitude, Mark is likely to be in a better position to have a more constructive conversation with John and potentially better understand the underlying reasons for the situation and come up with some workable solutions.

Easier said than done

Mark may go through the above exercise and identify the irrational belief and then the more constructive rational belief. However when it comes down to it, he may still feel that he cannot stand it and have the same resentment towards John which prevents him from feeling better and having a more constructive conversation.

Beliefs run deep. They have an amazing power over us. So how do we release the strong hold they have over us? How do we "enable" more rational beliefs that we identify? These are some techniques that can help:

a) Disputing them over and over again.

b) Acting against them over and over again.

Disputing them over and over can loosen them up. It is like taking their mask away so we can see them for what they truly are; unrealistic or exaggerated views of the world. Usually this is an important first step before we take action. Acting against our irrational beliefs is by far the most effective way to transform our learning from being emotional and momentary to being intellectual and lasting.

How Rational Thinking complements the Awareness Wheel

Rational thinking can also help us dispute those interpretations, assumptions, and opinions that are unrealistic and therefore cause us a great deal of stress. In Mark's case, he interpreted his boss's cancellation of the meeting as "she doesn't care about my professional development." This is irrational and unrealistic. Cancelling the meeting doesn't prove that his boss doesn't care. Mark might change this to "my interpretation is that she doesn't care" or "it is possible that she doesn't care, and it is possible that there are other reasons which I should explore." These are more realistic interpretations and they can help Mark explore other aspects of the wheel instead of being stuck in this interpretation.

Rational thinking can also help us replace rigid and unrealistic wants by softer and more realistic versions. So instead of holding on to "I want her to reschedule the meeting", it would be more realistic to change this to "I would like to reschedule the meeting, but if she doesn't, I can stand it and I can manage", and then move on to figuring out the best possible action.

When we go through the wheel and conclude that there isn't much that we can do about a situation, then rational thinking can help us accept the situation and let go of our childish belief that the situation "should" be different. Instead of holding on to the belief that "it should be different", we can replace it by a more realistic version which might acknowledge that "it would be nice if it was different, but even though it is the way it is, and it is inconvenient and undesirable, I can stand it and manage through it."

Third Technique: Being in the Present

If we are not in the "present", meaning not fully aware of what is going on right now, how can we make good decisions and have a positive impact on the future? Being in the present and noticing what is going on around us are pre-requisites for making better plans and better choices for the future. Not to mention that when we are in the present, we are likely to be more in touch with reality and not as subjected to irrational beliefs that can cause unnecessary stress. We are also likely to be more connected with the people around us and build better working relationships. All are ingredients for accomplishing a lot more with a lot less stress.

The past and the future are the making of our mind

It is easy to see how the future is the making of our mind. After all it hasn't happened yet. It is a projection that our mind creates about what it thinks will happen at some point in time. But how would you explain how the past is the making of our mind? That is because the "past" is what we remember from the past and not necessarily what actually happened in the past. Our memory unfortunately tends to be quite selective. Take a look at the Awareness Wheel again. When we remember a past situation, which parts of the Awareness Wheel do you think we are likely to remember?

It is more likely that we remember our interpretations, opinions, some of the feelings we experienced, and if we haven't identified our true wants at that time, we are likely to remember our superficial wants and whatever uninformed action we may have taken at the time. If Mark hadn't gone through the Awareness Wheel, he would have remembered that his boss "didn't care about his professional development and that he was really unhappy at work", and may have even drawn some additional irrational conclusions such as "bosses don't care" and "the workplace is really difficult and unfair."

If the past and the future are largely the making of our mind, doesn't it make sense to focus our energy on the present, and be more fully prepared to take better actions towards the future (instead of dwelling about the past or worrying about the future)?

Use the Awareness Wheel to be in the present

If you are still holding on to an event that happened in the past, find yourself preoccupied with it, and even stressed about it, the Awareness Wheel can help. Even if there is nothing that you can do about the event anymore, going through the wheel helps you shed some light on what really happened. You may be able to identify what your real wants were at the time, and what options you might have had. This can transform this past event from being an unpleasant or even daunting one to being a lesson learned. You can also "close" this issue and add it to the "closed issues" category in the catch-all to-do list in your Google Docs (described earlier in the book). Yet another way to expand the use of the catch-all to-do list!

As you can see the Awareness Wheel is multi-dimensional. It can be applied to current events that we need to address now. It can be applied to past events that are still unresolved in our mind. We can even apply it to potential future events that we are concerned about to feel better about them now and be proactive in preparing for them.

Exercise 1: Issues that are causing stress

Use this table to list the issues that are causing you stress and identify which of the above techniques is likely to help. Then after you apply the technique on each issue (using the diagrams detailed below), write down your comments and a brief description of the results.

Table 1: Issues that are causing stress

Issue	Techniques that is likely to help	Comment/Results

Exercise 2: Awareness Wheel

Issue: _____

_____

_____

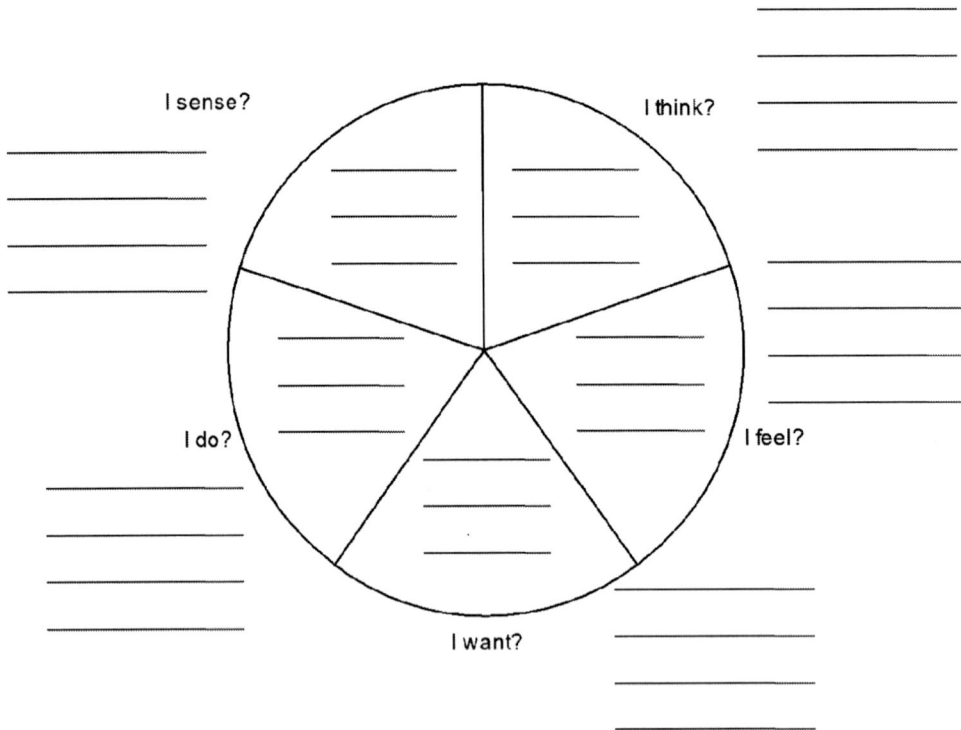

Exercise 3: Rational Thinking Diagram

Issue: _____

_____

_____

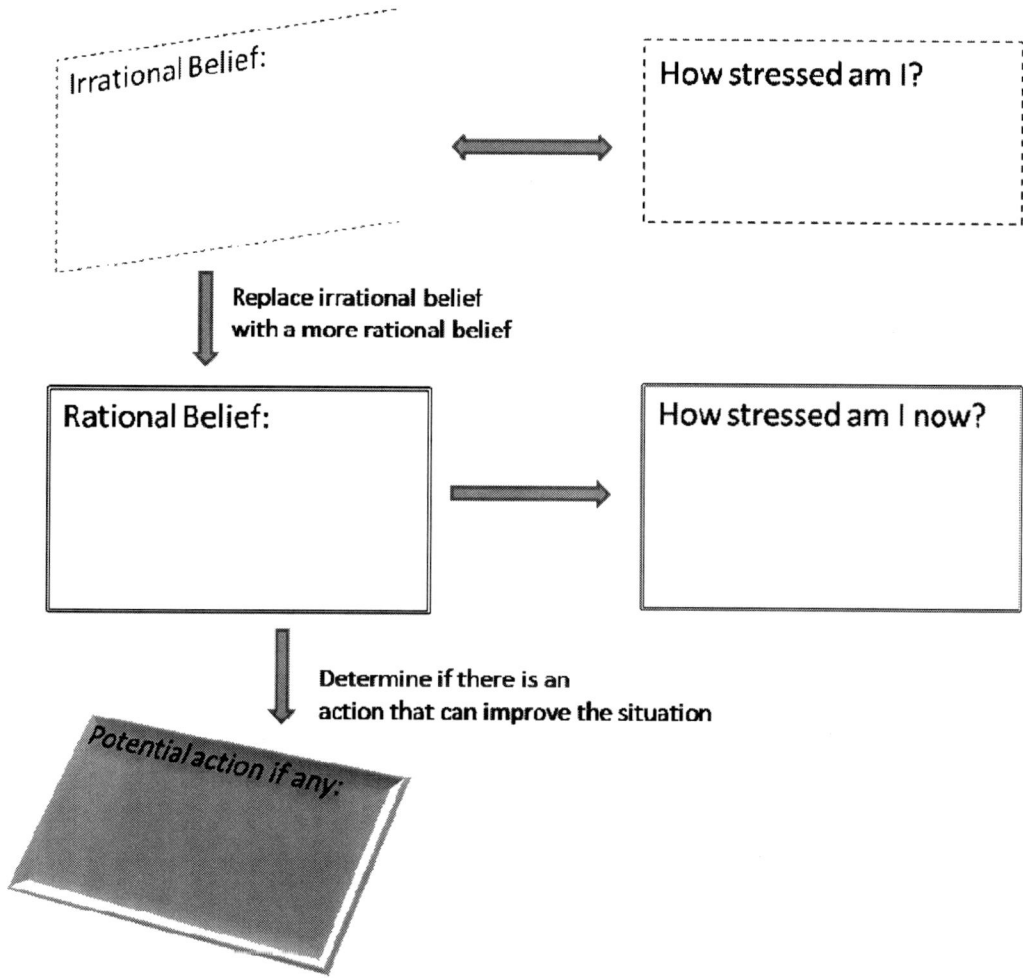

Irrational Belief:

How stressed am I?

Replace irrational belief
with a more rational belief

Rational Belief:

How stressed am I now?

Determine if there is an
action that can improve the situation

Potential action if any:

Action Plan

Identify the action items that you would like to take as a result of what was covered in this chapter. Indicate the timeframe in which you plan on taking these actions. Then report on the actual date in which you implemented them and a brief note about the results.

Table 2: Action Plan

Practice/Technique	I will start implementing this on (date?)	Actual start date	Actual end date	Comment/Results
Identify the issues that are causing you considerable stress				
Use the Awareness Wheel and/or the Rational Thinking Diagram to identify potential solutions				
Add your own item:				
Add your own item:				
Add your own item:				

Chapter 12: All wishful thinking until we take action

It is all wishful thinking until we take action. A lot happens when we take action! We discover and learn. We challenge the mind and the irrational beliefs that it holds on to. We set more constructive precedence for the future.

Why don't we take action?

If we know what to do, why don't we do it? Most of the time, we know what to do, but we still don't do it. Or we are capable of figuring out what to do, but we still don't put forth the necessary effort to figure it out. Scott Peck, the author of the Road Less Traveled, mentions laziness, fear, and pride, as the root causes of many of our troubles. I argue that they are the root causes behind our hesitation in taking action.

The paradox is that taking action helps dissolve laziness, uncover and dismantle our irrational beliefs behind the fear, and soften our pride. This is the "chicken and egg" theory. So how do we get started? How do we overcome the initial fear, laziness, and pride that is stopping us from getting the action started in the first place? Here are some ways we can get started:

1. Journaling about the action, and the reasons why the action is desirable, and what benefit it will bring.
2. Journaling about the irrational beliefs that may be preventing us from moving forward, disputing them, and formulating more rational and realistic views.
3. Visualizing and role playing in a safe environment.
4. Identifying small steps we can take to get started.
5. Finding a support system ranging from helpful resources to supportive friends and colleagues, to getting the help of a professional coach.
6. In some cases, it may be "just doing it" and challenging the laziness, fear, and pride. This involves tolerating the discomfort, only to find out soon, that the discomfort quickly goes away.

Turning the Accomplishing More With Less concepts and techniques into action

If you have already identified the actions that you want to take as a result of the Accomplishing More With Less Methodology by filling out your action plan at the end of each chapter, then formulating your final action plan below should be easy. If not, this is your opportunity to reflect on what you learned and come up with your action plan now.

Start with 3 easy actions or practices that you can implement right away, and one more challenging action or practice that is likely to take more planning and more implementation time. The 3 easy actions will give you some immediate benefits and get you motivated to do more. The more challenging action will give you more significant and sustainable results.

There are plenty of actions to choose from. Here is a list of what some of our workshop participants selected as their three easy actions or practices:

- Use e-mail labels to better manage unfinished messages.

- Start using the journal.

- Start the beginning of day reconciliation at the beginning of each day.

- Start the end of day reconciliation at the end of each day.

- Set up a catch-all to-do list in Google Docs to start to track all such items.

- Work in 40 minute focused sessions followed by collaborative sessions.

- Get a timer and use it to stay focused during the focused sessions.

- Starting micro-planning when working on an important task.

- Start to use the chat features with colleagues to minimize interruptions and help each other stay focused

- Incorporate purposeful breaks after each collaborative session and before the next focused session.

- Use the Immediate Priorities Matrix™ when you have many conflicting priorities, or every two weeks to plan more effectively.

Here are some examples of more challenging items that some of our workshop participants have chosen:

- Organize the filing structure and start using the new structure.

- Organize the desk.

- Empty the e-mail inbox.

- Negotiate with your team/boss/and other group members how to use chat to communicate to each other that you are focused and also discuss how to escalate issues when critical issues come up.

- Create a Google site to help my team better collaborate and share information instead of relying on e-mail.

- Use the End Results Matrix™ to identify the desired results for the next 3 to 6 months and then work at incorporating these activities into the schedule.

- Identify specific high-impact activities (that are part of the 20% effort that is bringing 80% of the results) and incorporate more of these activities into your schedule.

- Identify specific low-impact activities (that are part of the 80% effort that is only bringing minimal results) and do less of these activities.

- Select a difficult work or personal situation that is taking up a lot of time and energy, and using stress management techniques to identify the best possible action.

- Engage in further training and/or coaching activities to develop specific skills that will help accelerate your development.

Once you complete the above action plan, you will be motivated to take on the next step of actions, and this is the beginning of a whole new journey of growth, development, and accomplishment. Congratulations for having chosen this path!

Your Accomplishing more with less Action Plan

Table 1: Identify someone who can support you in this process (your informal coach)

Name	
E-mail	
Phone	

Table 2: List the three easy items, and dates you will get them done by

1.		
2.		
3.		

Table 3: List the more challenging item, and date you will get it done by

1.		
	Date/time on which you will spend 30 to 40 minutes to plan how you will get this done	

Your implementation checklist

- ☐ I executed the three easy items.
- ☐ I e-mailed my "coach" about having completed the three easy items.
- ☐ I scheduled my 30 to 40 minute session to plan my challenging item.
- ☐ I e-mailed my "coach" about my challenging item.
- ☐ I accomplished my challenging item.
- ☐ And don't forget to make use of the gift certificate that is provided to you with this book (see the introduction at the beginning of the book for the more details).

Date completed _____

CPSIA information can be obtained at www.ICGtesting.com
Printed in the USA
LVOW030354070312

271880LV00004B/16/P